<u>Everything is Possible</u>

Editing by: Nichola Daunton
Cover Design by: Filipe Roldao

Printed in the United Kingdom
First Printing, 2016
ISBN 978-1-326-56967-9
www.MartynSibley.com

DEDICATIONS

This is dedicated to my soul mate Kasia who has shared many of these adventures with me. This is also for my mum, dad, and sister for their unconditional love. Plus for all of my family and friends whose love/support/encouragement helped my dreams to come true. You know who you are anyway :-)

AKNOWLEDGEMENTS

There's so many people to thank for bringing this huge project together. Apologies if you didn't get a name check below, but you were equally important.

Firstly a big thank you to the Kickstarter crowdfunders. An amazing 65 people helped fund the costs of publishing this book. Without whom, the book would still be in my head and not down on paper. Paper full of words for others to use and enjoy. A huge fistbump goes to all of the disabled people (and their families and friends) who inspired and informed me on how to live a fulfilling life. I hope this book does the same to many others in the future.

A massive thank you goes to my friend and editor, Nichola Daunton, for our long chats about what to include and not to include. Her literary knowledge and expertise has made this book happen. Also thanks to the omnipresent Filipe Roldao for his book design and general support. I think you'll agree the cover is fantastic. Last, but not least, to Jon Morely for his much appreciated input and advice.

A few others deserve a hat tip too. AJ and Melissa Leon from Misfit Inc mentored me into blogging - it's amazing to look back at what I've achieved since starting my blog. My friend Srin Madipalli and I created Disability Horizons and Accomable together. The vast impact made, the team members and their communities deserve lots of gratitude. Also charities like Scope and SMA Support UK have been hugely helpful on this journey. As have Carrie-Ann from Tourism for All, and Ivor Ambrose from the European Network for Accessible Tourism. Plus all the many other professionals, organisations and tourist boards along the way. Collaboration always wins the day!

CONTENTS

BONUS BONANZA

Before you get settled in to reading about my background, barriers and beautiful adventures, there's one more thing to mention. Having doubted, struggled, and questioned so many things myself in the past, this book is to help you through these exact same moments.

In knowing that others found solutions and success gives us all hope. In understanding HOW they did it gives us a pathway and new tools. There's plenty of inspiration and information in this book, but I wanted to give you much more.

To thank you so much for taking the time to read my book, and as a way of expressing my gratitude, I've put together some bonuses for you:

1. Exciting full colour photos of all my adventures.

2. All of the videos mentioned in the book too.

Check them out here:
www.MartynSibley.com/EverythingIsPossibleBook

Chapter One - The Biographical Bit

"Birth of the Baby Milk Boy"

Hello, my name's Martyn Sibley, and like most autobiographies, mine begins with a lot of screaming and a birth. When I was born, way back in the mists of time, or 1983 to be precise, I was born with a rare genetic condition called SMA or Spinal Muscular Atrophy. Being born with SMA (type II if you want to get technical about it) wasn't exactly random potluck, because although my parents didn't know it at the time, they both carried a faulty SMN1 gene, which meant that any child they had together would have a 1 in 4 chance of being born with some variant of the condition.

My parents had met while they were both working in the insurance business at General Accident in Cambridge, not far from where they eventually settled together near the little town of St Ives - which is sadly often overshadowed by its much hipper namesake in Cornwall; and after a wedding, a honeymoon and a few years interlude, I was welcomed into the world on the 3rd September 1983.

To most people, SMA is a popular brand of baby milk formula and nothing more, but to those of us who are familiar with or have the condition, SMA means Spinal Muscular Atrophy, a group of conditions of which there are four types (I, II, III and IV– very creatively!). In simple terms, Spinal Muscular Atrophy is a genetic disease that leads to various levels of muscle weakness depending on the type the person has. This muscle weakness, caused by the deterioration of the motor neurones which connect the brain and the spinal cord, means that people with SMA often have trouble with sitting up, walking, and as a baby, crawling. How exactly SMA affects you depends on the type you have, with type I being the most severe. For me, SMA meant that I got my first electric wheelchair at the age of 3 and needed to be carried around a lot as a baby and a toddler as my movement was restricted. Although it is necessary for me to explain my condition so you have a bit of context, this book isn't about SMA. It isn't even really about being disabled, though obviously that is a major part of my life. It is about overcoming challenges and realizing what you can achieve, whatever you feel is holding you back.

So now the science bit is over, lets get back to my family. After putting lots of thought into it, my parents decided to have another child, despite now being aware that this child would also have a 1 in 4 chance of being born with SMA too. Though this obviously added a bit more stress than usual to the pregnancy, my parents were as prepared as they could be for any eventuality and Claire Sibley (Claire Bear to her friends and family) came kicking and screaming into the world. The fact that Claire was kicking, screaming and moving around from the very beginning soon proved to my parents that she didn't have SMA, as I had been the complete opposite as a baby. Though it is interesting to note, that while everyone therefore assumed Claire would be the one who would be the most curious and keen to explore the world, it is actually me who has been the one eager to go travelling and explore new places, whereas Claire is a self-confessed home bird. Stereotypes eh!

So with Claire's birth, our little family unit of four was complete (though it was to increase in ways we couldn't yet imagine) and it was time for me to take the plunge and start school.

"The Only Disabled in the Village"

St Ives and the surrounding villages are small, and at this point in its history I was well and truly "the only disabled in the village". Zipping around in my electric wheelchair from the age of 3 years old, I think you can imagine that I was a hard kid to ignore. But whereas in some places in the world, being the only disabled person might bring negative attention, in St Ives I couldn't have been more at home. Whether I was playing football with my friends (dribbling the ball on my foot rest) or enlisting the fastest kid in town to go and catch the girl of my childhood dreams during a game of kiss chase, all the kids at my school, Holywell Primary, treated me just like any other kid. That's the great thing about children, unless you teach them that something is weird, or let your prejudices rub off on them, generally they'll treat everyone exactly the same. All they need is a short explanation of why someone is in a wheelchair or has a disability, and they'll just except it and get on with it.

At school, I was lucky enough to be very well catered for, with a number of excellent LSA's (Learning Support Assistants) at my disposal. This meant I never missed out on anything, and that I got exactly the same level of education as everyone else in my class. In a different environment, I'm well aware that being the only disabled child in my school, and indeed the whole village, could've been a very lonely experience for me. But as everyone in the village treated me just the same as everybody else, despite the extra help I often needed, I never had to define myself by my disability and I never internalized it in the way that I otherwise might. I'm sure, that just like anyone who feels different (and who doesn't at some point?) I must've wondered "why me?" but these feelings did not define my childhood and I generally felt happy and settled in my life and at my school. As I worked my way towards the end of primary school though, all this would change.

"The Special Bus"

"Inaccessible". If you're disabled or have a mobility issue, you'll have heard that word more times that you care to remember. Sadly, the UK, like many other countries around the world, still have a long way to go when it comes to accessibility and ensuring public spaces are open to all. At the age of 11 I'd no doubt already experienced my fair share of inaccessible buildings, but this didn't affect me on such a gut-wrenching level until I was unable to go to the same secondary school as all of my friends.

All of a sudden, my disability was stopping me from doing something that I really wanted to do. The school was inaccessible, and no amount of learning support would enable me to go there. The world I had felt so safe and secure in had been ripped from under my wheels and I would have to go to a secondary school 16 miles away in the neighbouring village of Impington. Even worse, I would have to get on the "special bus" every morning to get there. The "special bus" was an accessible bus full of other disabled children who also had to travel from the surrounding villages of Cambridgeshire to attend Impington Village College. As the only disabled kid in my area, I hadn't really been around other disabled people before, so being thrown into the world of disability and all that it entailed was something of a culture shock to 11 year old me. Suddenly I was made conscious of my own disability and all the negative stereotypes, restrictions and connotations that came with it. Needless to say, I wasn't happy. Leaving all your friends behind to attend a school where you know no one is tough for any child, but being suddenly lumbered with the awareness that the reason for this is that you're "different" and your difference can't always be accommodated, adds another level of confusion, frustration and sadness to the mix.

While it certainly look me a while to adjust to getting on the "special bus" every morning and all that this implied about my life and the limitations that were being placed on me, ultimately going to a different school than my friends and meeting other disabled people for the first time, was a very positive and life-changing experience. As I hurtled towards my teenage years, being surrounded by other disabled people who also needed help going to the toilet or needed to use a bottle to pee, meant that I felt less alone in these specific experiences of life. Experiences that none of my peers at primary school had needed to deal with. For the first time, I was more aware of my own disability in a wider societal context, and while I still felt just like one of the gang back in St Ives, I was also able to feel at home among other disabled people who were experiencing things my non-disabled friends would never quite understand. Truth be told, looking back I was lucky enough to have the best of both worlds, and to learn about, and learn to deal with my disability in a way that didn't put any restrictions on me until I was old enough to deal with them.

Not being able to go to the school that I wanted to wasn't the only thing that my disability impacted on during my childhood though. Travel was another area that was affected. Although at first it was my parents who had to deal with the the ins and outs of accessible travel, while I remained blissfully unaware.

"Wish You Were Here? (Minus Judith Chalmers)"

One of my first trips abroad was on a family holiday to Florida at the tender age of 4, minus the yet to be born Claire Bear. As I was so young, I have very little memory of the flight, the hotel, or much of the holiday at all, except for the fact that this is where I first learnt to swim. As you'll see throughout the rest of this book, swimming has continued to be an important part of my life, and in terms of exercise it is particularly good for people with SMA.

As I was still a very small child at the time, my parents didn't have to source an accessible hotel for the trip, as they carried me everywhere I needed to go within the apartment, while my electric wheelchair was only used outside. Though I have since learnt, from talking to my parents, that getting my electric wheelchair onto the plane was quite a difficult task, and this is something that still causes a lot of problems when I have travelled abroad to this day.

Once we were there though, learning to swim was a big step for me, and shows how keen my parents were for me to have as normal a life as any other young child. There is even still video footage of my dad supporting me through my first ever length without armbands! The older I got though, the more complex my needs became, and as I started to use an electric wheelchair indoors as well, sourcing accessible accommodation abroad became more of a struggle. Plus with another child to look after as well, my parents decided to take us on a lot of holidays within Britain instead. So Norfolk, Brighton and Bournemouth featured heavily in my childhood, like they probably did in the childhoods of most kids growing up in 80's and 90's England. For now, the glamour and glitz of that magical place "abroad" was confined mostly to the TV, with Judith Chalmers and Jill Dando sauntering around endlessly glamorous locations for us all to gawp at on shows like *Wish You Were Here?* and *Holiday.* A personal favourite of mine at the time though was Michael Palin and his travel documentaries for the BBC, especially shows like *Pole to Pole* (1992) and *Full Circle With Michael Palin* (1997). Watching Palin explore all these new and wonderful places, all of which seemed a million miles away from flat and grey Cambridgeshire, filled me with a desire to get out there and see the world, and made me feel, for the first time, that I'd quite like to be in front of the camera presenting travel documentaries of my own…

Back in Blighty though, I was getting to know the British Isles and family holidays during my childhood were happy affairs, full of laughter, board games and shivering at the seaside, like all the best traditional British holidays. By the time I was 10 years old though, my parents had decided that their marriage was no longer working and that they should get a divorce. While divorce obviously isn't easy for any family, my parents made sure that we kids had a healthy and happy relationship with both of them. Claire and I continued to live with Mum and Dad equally, as they both still lived locally.

So, on the precipice of my teens, not only did I have a new family dynamic, I was also at a new school with a whole group of new people – and while they say a change is as good as a holiday, I was about to get the best of both worlds.

"Teenage Kicks"

After many years of "staycations", we started going abroad more, but this time with my stepdad Dave and my stepbrothers Robbie and Jamie in tow, all of whom were welcome editions to our expanding family. We were soon jetting off on a series of holidays to the Canary Islands. As I was older by this point, I have a lot more vivid memories of the trouble my Mum had to go to in order to source accessible hotels, equipment and adapted taxis. On the lead up to our holidays I'd overhear a lot of phone calls trying to source these things, but with my Mum's positive and can-do attitude, she never gave up, and even when things failed to work out as expected when we got there, with her great gift for problem-solving she'd soon have everything sorted, whether people were being helpful or not. On one particular holiday, I remember her walking up and down a massive hill in Tenerife three times in one morning in order to source a shower chair and a hoist that would be appropriate for me. What a star!

This is of course a book about adventurous travel. So it makes sense to focus on the bigger trips abroad, of which I remember more about the older I became. However I want to add that Claire and I enjoyed some great holidays with my dad and his new family too. Modern family trees are more like orchards these days. Needless to say my dad was also great at organising trips to Norfolk, Weymouth and Gran Canaria over my teen years. I owe a lot to mum and dad for their support.

So these holidays in the Canaries, particularly in my later teen years of 15-19, were a real turning point for me. Due to my condition, I am prone to getting chest infections, which then put me at risk of developing pneumonia, in the winter months. Travelling to the Canaries in these months gave me a new lease of life and meant I got a much-needed break from the cold hands and feet and weakness that came with a British winter. Having Jamie and Robbie by my side was great too, especially when we slapped on the Joop! and went out to explore Tenerife's nightlife. Having the freedom to leave my Mum and Stepdad behind, and go out and explore the pubs and clubs on a warm summer evening, gave me my first real taste of freedom, as well as my first real taste of the joy of meeting new people and learning about new cultures.

While I loved going abroad, at this point in my life I found flying a pretty traumatic experience. The first flight I was properly aware of was when I was around 10 years old, and from then on, until the age of 16, I was very scared of flying. If you're disabled, boarding a plane isn't easy, and the struggle to keep control of the situation starts from the moment you check in. Most airlines want to take your wheelchair off of you and put you in a manual chair when you check in your luggage, but as I am unable to sit in a chair without proper head support for that amount of time, I have to firmly insist that I have to stay in my chair, which is sometimes met with understanding and sometimes with confusion. They then check in the chair anyway, but allow me to stay in it until it is time for boarding. Then at the boarding gate, I'm lifted out of my chair, which is then taken to the hold, while I am put in an aisle chair. This is a narrow seat that I am transferred into by the handles of a special transit seat – basically a sling with handles – that I have been sitting on since the morning. The aisle chair is then tipped backwards onto its back wheels in order to get up the plane steps (as most planes still don't have a ramp option) and then I am wheeled to my seat and transferred via the sling yet again. From here on in, I'm stuck in my plane seat until the end of the flight, so there's no question of being able to use the toilet. I either have to take a bottle and try and cover myself for privacy, or wear a 'leg bag', which then has to be discreetly emptied for me during the flight. On longer flights, I'm sure you can imagine that

case of at least one assistant Jon Morely (who'll you'll be hearing much more about later) life-long friendships were formed.

So after initial nerves, fears and trepidations, my time at university was AMAZING. Not only could I now stay out until 2am and get drunk without my parents having to put me to bed, I also actually enjoyed the work! Who knew! Not only that, I also met so many interesting and new people from all around the world, especially as during my second year the charity CSV took over the care support scheme and started recruiting care volunteers from across Europe and the wider world. During my first year, with the assistance of Motability and the good people of St Ives who raised a lot of money for me to get an adapted car, I also learnt to drive, which opened up the world to me even more and has proved invaluable to my travels ever since.

I could spend the rest of this chapter telling you a lot of juicy stories about all the naughty things I got up to while I was in Cov, but this isn't that kind of autobiography (read Katie Price's if you want those kind of stories!). So I think it's time I finished uni, with my BA in Economics in hand (and Masters Degree still to come), and set off on my first major travel adventure, don't you?

Chapter Two - Australia

"Becoming a culture vulture"

After three years away from home I was a different man, well sort of. There can be no doubt that university expanded my horizons in more ways than I had anticipated. Not only did I learn to study independently, I also learnt to manage my own budget (you'd hope so given that I was studying economics, wouldn't you?) and to cope with receiving care from a wide range of people, most of whom had never had a care job before. As the charity who recruited PA's for the university, CSV, recruited them from around the world, I was introduced to people from countries I'd never visited and from cultures I'd never learnt about. From China to Columbia, via Austria and Poland, meeting so many people helped me to see the world from new perspectives and amplified my desire to get out there and visit all these countries myself.

While I was by no means a fully-fledged adult by the time I finished university (are we ever?) I was feeling much more confident, and I was still youthful enough to have a fearless and adventurous spirit. For me though, it wasn't just a case of jetting off on a spur of the moment holiday as soon as I finished my finals. When you have a disability and you're planning to go away on your own for the first time (or as alone as you can be with two PA's in tow) there's a lot of planning that needs to happen before you can get anywhere near an airport. Planning which for me, started a full year before takeoff.

"If you're going to aim, aim high"

Sydney, Australia. Not only is it on the other side of the world, 10,566.67 miles from London Heathrow if you want to be exact, it's also a pretty big challenge to set yourself if you're a disabled person and you've never been on holiday without your parents. Which is of course, was exactly why I wanted to do it.

Whether you want to put it down to the fearlessness of youth or a desire to prove myself, Australia was where I was determined to go for my first "solo" trip abroad. There was some thought behind it too though. Thought that went beyond the babes in bikinis and the glittering sandy beaches I'd grown up watching on *Neighbours* and *Home and Away.* Not only was Australia an English speaking country, it was also highly developed just like England and had a similar culture and cuisine. To this day, there are still many more developing areas of the world such as parts of Africa and Asia that I would love to travel to, but given the lack of accessible infrastructure and medical assistance, I am hesitant to go, given the challenges that I would inevitably face upon arrival.

The fact that Australians have similar culinary tastes to us Brits was very important to me, as I was, and still am to an extent, a very fussy eater. At the age of 15 I had a major operation (my spine was fused with two titanium rods following a large spinal curvature and consequential breathing difficulties). As a result of being in hospital for so long, I eventually dropped down to as low as 4.5 stone. So by the time I finished uni I was still very thin. As I've already mentioned, I also had a tendency to get physically sick when nervous, and although this got better as I got older, my relationship with food was still quite a nervous one when I finished my degree. I was very particular about what I would and wouldn't eat. As a result, the thought of eating food in another country was a big deal to me, and a source of real stress. What would the food be like? Would it be different? Would I like it? And if I didn't, what would I eat? All of these issues were going round and round in my head, so choosing somewhere like Australia felt like a safe bet, food wise at least. The fact it was on the other side of the globe was another issue entirely.

Jon, one of my original PA's from my first year at Coventry, had continued to live and work in the area and we had remained friends. So it was Jon who I originally began discussing the idea of Australia with, and spurred on by his enthusiasm and encouragement, I began floating the idea with friends and family in 2004. A full year before we would eventually get there. I have noticed since then, that this is how many of my grand schemes begin, by being shared and discussed with my close circle of friends and relatives. Supportive voices who I know will give me an honest opinion and will help out if they can. If you're going for this approach in your own life though, it is important to realise that some people will be pessimistic about your hopes and dreams no matter how small or outlandish they are, so it's important to learn what advice is helpful and what is just designed to hold you back. Some people might see this as foolhardiness on my part, but by remaining positive I believe you can achieve a hell of a lot more than if you let people's negative opinions in. Though of course it is important to be realistic too. If I were trying to go into space by wheelchair, it'd be down right stupid of me to ignore people who said it wasn't possible with today's technology.

All in all then, it took a full year to plan the Australia trip, and boy was there a lot to plan. Not only did we have to source accessible hotels, accessible taxis, and find flights with an appropriate airline, I also had to find the right care team and work out exactly how I was going to fund my own trip, let alone pay for my PA's.

Although this all seemed a bit overwhelming at first, we soon managed to recruit some specialist help in the form of a travel agent named Jos who worked in my hometown of St. Ives. While many travel agents at this time (and probably still now) weren't clued up about disability and accessible travel, Jos was most definitely a diamond in the rough. Empathetic, understanding and brimming with contacts, she helped us to plan most of the holiday, sourcing accessible hotels, booking our flights from Heathrow and our internal flights around Oz. In other words, big shout out to Jos! While I've now learnt to do most of this stuff myself, having someone else there to help really made us all feel more confident about what we were getting ourselves into, and made everything seem far more plausible than it initially had. If I was trying to be funny, and if she'd been a man I would've called her my "Wizard of Oz" but that would just be too terrible a joke wouldn't it?

"Who wants a free(ish) trip to Australia?"

Though Jon was on board from the start, we quickly came to the conclusion that he'd need some help and wouldn't be able to provide all of my care alone. Especially for the three weeks we were planning to go for. We initially recruited another former PA from

Cov to share the load, but unfortunately he dropped out halfway through the planning stage. So who could we find to replace him?

Looking around for someone new, I hit upon the idea of getting in contact with one of my former LSA's from secondary school, who had helped me out when I'd gone on a school trip to Devon and Cornwall aged 15. Emma had been younger than the rest of the LSA's, and while she was obviously older than both Jon and me, she was familiar with my care and up for an adventure. I was very keen to have someone I'd worked with before, as having to deal with training at such short notice, or indeed on the holiday itself, would have taken its toll on us all.

With two PA's now firmly in place, it was time to sort out the delicate but very critical question of money. Which is where things get a little bit complicated! Since the age of 18 I'd been receiving 'Direct Payments' in order to fund my care in term time, so I'd been able to save some money up from the holidays. Plus on top of that, this was the old days before the financial crash and all the cuts in local council funding, when Respite Funding was still very much a thing – a fund that existed solely to give disabled people the chance to get away from the daily grind and relieve their full time carers.

The idea of such a fund existing today is almost laughable considering how far the cuts have gone, but as the chair of SMA Supports Adult Insight Group we have been campaigning for the charity to create its own respite fund in order to help pay for the extra costs of care and equipment. I firmly believe that this type of funding shouldn't be seen as a luxury, and should be available at least once to anyone who needs it.

On top of my Disability Living Allowance (paid for the recognised higher costs of living for disabled people) I had also been in receipt of Severe Disablement Allowance (SDA) since I turned 16, which was available to me as long as I stayed in education. So with the DLA and the SDA that I'd managed to save up over the past few years covering my costs, combined with the Respite Funding and ongoing Direct Payments I decided it would be wise to strike a deal with Jon and Emma in order to get this show on the road. It was important to make sure that everyone knew where they stood financially.

With the money saved, I was able to buy all of their plane tickets and also cover most of Jon and Emma's other costs, though not all. In return, they would provide my care, and while they wouldn't end up with any money in their bank accounts at the end of the trip, they would get to see Australia basically for free. They both agreed to this deal, and although I would still have to cover my own costs, we could just about manage it if we all shared a hotel room. This would involve me and Jon top and tailing and Emma sleeping on a camp bed. It wasn't ideal, but hey, it was Australia!

As Jon and Emma had never met before, despite growing up in roughly the same area, I was a bit concerned as to how they would get on. Unless you're going away on holiday, it is rare for your different PA's to have to spend much time together. This though was going to be a solid three weeks, with long journeys, cramped living conditions and alcohol all thrown into the mix. It was possible things could get complicated, precisely how complicated I couldn't have anticipated...

"Healthy body, healthy mind"

As I mentioned in the first chapter, one of the main issues of living with SMA is getting through the winter in one piece. In January of that year I'd nearly been hospitalised with pneumonia, which meant I'd had nearly two months off of uni. On top of that, a week or two before we were due to fly to Oz, I developed a niggling chesty cough, so I had to pack emergency antibiotics in my suitcase in case it got worse. Although I knew how quickly any cough could develop into a chest infection and then potentially pneumonia, nothing was going to stop me getting on that plane. From my mum's perspective though, this wasn't exactly easy. My going to university had been stressful enough for her, and although she was proud of my ambition and drive, I knew she wouldn't be at ease until I was back in England safe and sound.

Despite her worry, I'd included Mum in the planning of the trip from the very beginning and she'd been instrumental, as she'd been the one to introduce me to Jos. Sometimes I think it would be easier for my Mum if I didn't tell her my next grand plan, but having her support, no matter how cautious she is at first, has always been very important to me.

"Hey ho, let's go!"

By the time we were finally ready to set off for the airport, my nerves were going full throttle. The plan was to fly from Heathrow to Singapore, stay the night and then fly on to Sydney the next morning. After weeks of worrying what to pack we all bundled into the car, me in my transfer seat ready to get on the plane, and we were off! It wasn't until we were sitting having a coffee at Heathrow that I actually got true butterflies in my stomach, because finally, after a long year of planning I allowed myself to think 'yeah, we're actually doing this!'

The flight to Singapore was over 11 hours long, eg; not fantastic if you're disabled and can't go to the toilet. While I could discreetly use my bottle with a little bit of modesty from Emma and Jon blocking the view, going for a 'number two' was out of the question and obviously going against nature isn't good for anyone's insides. I think it was my sheer determination to get to Oz that saw me through this though. That and going to the toilet as close to the flight time as possible at Heathrow, and as soon as I possibly could at the airport in Singapore. While it's generally not a hot topic for group discussion (well, not among my friends anyway), it is these kinds of things that put many disabled people off travelling, especially over such long distances.

After a long 11 hours, a lot of bad movies and a few fretful snoozes, we finally touched down in Singapore. One of the first things that hit us about Singapore, and it felt like it was quite literally hitting us, was the heat. Compared to the British July weather that'd we'd left behind, the humidity levels were intense, but there's nothing like a dramatic change in temperature to make you feel like you're on holiday. After collecting my wheelchair and our luggage, we were finally out of the airport and onto the incredibly clean streets of Singapore. This was another marked difference from the chewing gum studded streets of England, as everything here was immaculately clean because chewing gum had been banned since 2004 (except for therapeutic use apparently!).

Once we'd left the airport we were swept through the clean streets by our very friendly accessible taxi driver, who gave us a tour of the city and eventually dropped us off in Chinatown. Now it was time to test my food fears and order something to eat from a street vendor. Thankfully though, so as not to stretch my taste buds too far, they had a very tasty looking chicken curry, one of my firm favourites, though my Mum had certainly never served it to me on the big green leaf that I was now given as a plate. I definitely felt like I was on foreign soil now!

When it comes to being in a wheelchair, it is always interesting to see how people in different countries react to me, though up until this point I hadn't had much experience of this. This was the first time I'd been in a country, where as a white man I was most definitely a minority, while as a disabled white man, I felt like a double minority. Many people stopped and stared at me in the street turning around and following us down the road. It was certainly an odd feeling to experience, though by no means a threatening one. While it would be easy for me to be offended, you have to account for the fact that many people have never seen a disabled person out of the house before in some countries, let alone seen an electric wheelchair in action, especially with someone else riding on the back!

After polishing off our food it was time to head back to the hotel, where we'd dropped off our luggage earlier. As we were only staying for one night we'd decided to forgo the hassle of tracking down, hiring and paying for a hoist, so Emma and Jon had to lift me onto the toilet and onto the bed. This isn't a common experience for me, so it was quite scary at first, but under the circumstances it was the easiest thing to do. With jet lag and confused body clocks we were all pretty knackered by this point and the small hotel room wasn't going to stop us from getting some much needed sleep before the next flight to Sydney in the morning.

"From Singapore to Sydney"

After clocking up another 9 hours in the sky with the second flight, by the time we arrived in Sydney it was morning again and our body clocks were well and truly scrambled. When we eventually made it to the hotel, the Australian equivalent of a Travelodge, once again with a shared room for the three of us, Emma unfortunately had a migraine and had to take herself off to bed for a good portion of the day. Despite being very tired though, Jon and me were far too excited to go to bed too, and so we went out for a walk and our first proper view of Sydney.

Walking (and rolling) in the Botanical Gardens on a sunny morning of about 20 degrees, we got our first proper view of the Harbor Bridge and the Sydney Opera House - two iconic symbols of Australia that made me feel like we'd well and truly arrived. In the gardens we also had a serious chat about how everyone was coping so far. Both Jon and me were worried that if Emma was finding things difficult, then we were going to run into problems further down the line. We decided at this point though to just see how things panned out and take it one day at a time, as opposed to having any sort of group discussion about it right now. We both realised that it had been a very long trip so far and perhaps we all just needed a few days to recover before we were all back on peak form again.

At this point we didn't have a strict itinerary in place, so when Emma was feeling better later in the afternoon, we all met up in a nearby coffee shop and read some magazines to work out what was happening in the city that week. At this point in my life, at the tender age of 21, I was definitely much more interested in going out and cruising during the evenings, having a few drinks, meeting new people and hitting the clubs. Although we wanted to experience some of Sydney's cultural hotspots, having fun and drinking were

31

definitely at the top of the list, a lot more so than they are now, a decade or so later. While we chilled in the coffee bar we discovered that one of my favourite bands at the time, The Roots (famous for The Seed 2.0), were playing in Sydney in a few days time, so we booked tickets and continued to hunt for more cool places.

The nightlife, and the surreal situations we ended up in because of it, is what I remember most about Sydney. As Emma was a bit older than both Jon and me, she wasn't as keen to go out drinking and clubbing every night, so often it was just the two of us cruising around the city looking for a good time. Sadly, I didn't find the Aussie youth as friendly and approachable as I'd expected them to be (perhaps the idyllic vision painted by *Neighbours* and *Home and Away* wasn't so realistic after all!) and we sometimes had trouble finding out where the cool clubs actually were. There are a few nights that have really stuck in my mind though, including the time Jon and me stumbled across the Gas Nightclub (which has sadly now closed down). After queuing up in the long line that snaked around the side of the club, we were told upon getting to the front, that there was no access at the main entrance so we'd have to go through the back. The back happened to be a very creepy, dark and dingy multi-storey car park with an old fashioned, hand-operated metal lift that we had to take to the very bottom of the building. Fearing ever so slightly for our lives we came out of the lift, went through some dark doors and found ourselves in a huge underground Hip Hop club full of people of Chinese origins sitting at tables and sipping expensive champagne. This was definitely not what we were expecting, but it was a very welcome surprise after the creepy journey in.

In another surreal and rather sinister moment, in a bar later in the week, a man came up to our group (this time including Emma) and told me that he wanted to take me onto the roof, break my legs and rape me. Whether this was a strange type of Australian humour, an awkward attempt at a joke, or a real threat, it certainly wasn't a comfortable experience. I'm not sure whether this hinted at larger attitudes to disabled people in the country, or whether he was just the usual type of crazy man that you get in bars anywhere in the world. Throughout Australia though, the access was good and most buildings that we wanted to access catered for disabled people. Though I didn't see that many disabled people out on the streets, in those days I was less in tune with the social model of disability and I wasn't specifically looking for disabled people either.

"There's no such thing as a free lunch"

Overall though, Sydney was a laidback and generally friendly city, though we didn't get to know as many of the locals as we perhaps wanted to. When it came to the care situation though, things were not going as well as I'd hoped they would. As I mentioned before, Jon and Emma hadn't met before we went away and unfortunately there was a definite personality clash. From the beginning, Jon felt that he had done more than his fair share of the care work. For example at the airport, in the clubs and when Emma had come down with a migraine.

This then set the scene for the week to come, and although I had originally intended it to work on a day on, day off shift pattern, as Jon was much more keen than Emma to go out and socialise, he often came out with us when Emma was working, as well as on the nights he was working too. Although Emma had clearly been more affected by the stresses of travelling than either me or Jon, we were all pretty frazzled during the first week and this pushed us all to a particularly climatic moment during a meal out towards the end of our week in Sydney.

One of my best and oldest friends Billy, also of St Ives fame, had been travelling in Australia for a few months prior to our arrival and was about to head back to the UK. Before leaving though, he met up with us for a few days in Sydney, and I decided to treat everyone to a meal at my expense, as a way of saying thank you for helping me to achieve this lifetime ambition. It was at this point that I wondered if Emma hadn't been as happy with the payment deal as she had perhaps let on. She possibly took my gesture further by ordering more, when everyone else had stuck to a basic meal. In the end, both Billy and Jon ended up chipping in when the bill came, as it was so quite expensive for my means, and after the meal Billy decided to take Emma to one side and talk to her about the situation. While this wasn't comfortable for any of us, least of all Emma, who felt terrible, from this point onwards she was much better, although clearly not as relaxed as she initially had been. Although I didn't know it at the time, this taught me a vital lesson about managing my PA's and ensuring that everyone knows exactly where they stand and what the limits and the rules are from the very beginning. I'm sure Emma understands why this anecdote and lesson was important to share. We all live and learn.

With things finally settled, our week in Sydney was coming to a close and it was time to pack our bags once again and get our first internal flight south to Melbourne.

"Everybody needs good Neighbours"

The wonderful Jos had arranged all our internal flights as well as our flights to and from Australia, so the flight to Melbourne went as smoothly as could be expected. Upon landing though, we looked out of the window to the runway below and saw the baggage staff pulling bits off my wheelchair. Acting quickly, we had to get the cabin crew to run down and tell them to stop immediately as the chair obviously had to stay as one unit if I was going to get back into it! This was a hairy moment, but since then I've almost got used to the fact that airports seem to find it extremely difficult to cope with wheelchairs, and accepted that it is going to be a constant battle.

After this "little" incident though, we were out of the airport and into the, well, blistering cold. In all my excitement while planning the trip I had failed to take into account the temperature difference between Sydney and Melbourne, and the fact that while Sydney's winter was relatively mild and more like our spring, Melbourne's was a touch more frosty in feeling. In fact, unluckily for us, it was about to snow for the first time in 50 years.

As you know by now, I really struggle in cold weather, so in Melbourne the wild night life was put on hold and our new routine consisted of going to a brand of coffee bars called Gloria Jeans and getting toast and hot chocolate. Quite different from rolling around the streets of Sydney until the small hours looking for bars, babes, and music.

On top of all this, and possibly because of it, Jon came down with a bad flu-like cold. This meant I spent a bit more time with Emma during this period, which helped to balance things out. Swings and roundabouts eh. We had fun bumbling around the city and going for Greek and Italian dinners, which happen to be two of my culinary favourites. Melbourne seemed a lot richer in culture in general, and if you can call it culture, one of the first museums we went to contained sets from everyone's favourite Australian soap opera, *Neighbours.* Although Ramsey Street itself was a bit too far out in the sticks for us to get to, seeing these sets was a real treat for the child in me, and we had great fun posing in the Robinsons' kitchen. We also took a look at Melbourne Cricket Ground, and on his day off Jon visited Melbourne's Aboriginal Museum and came back so enthusiastic and worked up about what the Aboriginal people had been put through, that I visited the museum myself the next day. Jon went on to do lots of research about everything he'd learnt, and used this research for his PhD later in the year.

On another day we took a trip to the hip and trendy district of St Kilda, home to an Aussie Rules football team and Luna Park, an old-fashioned theme park. A seaside resort, St Kilda would have been a better place to visit at the height of summer, but it was still a very cool place to hang out, and we managed to find a great restaurant where we could snuggle up next to an open fire and enjoy some great food.

This was most certainly a slower-paced trip than Sydney had been, but nonetheless we still managed to run into some surreal situations. One evening, Jon and me were out cruising the streets, when we heard that that there was an African Beauty Pageant happening in a nearby neighbourhood. As we were at a loose end and Jon was studying Caribbean Literature for his PhD, we decided to go and check it out. Going to a beauty pageant in the middle of winter, in the middle of Australia was certainly a strange experience, but it is the strange experiences that stick with you and end up being some of the most memorable moments of any trip.

On another equally memorable night, I almost started a fight with a bloke in a bar in a supposedly rough part of town. After having so much trouble trying to make friends with the younger locals, me and Jon struck up a conversation with an Aussie couple in their 50's named Neville and Wendy. After chatting about the UK and Oz for half an hour, they asked us what we were up to next and we asked them if they could recommend any local nightspots. They suggested a few places, but told us to definitely avoid the nightclub opposite us, which was well known for its rough reputation and had apparently been the location for a spate of stabbings. Well of course, after this warning, there was nowhere we wanted to go more! We headed straight for the club, ordered our drinks, ordered some more, and before I knew it, I was grabbing a guy who had been rude to us by his leather jacket and telling him to F off. Thankfully for us he was shocked by my behaviour and did actually, well head off, but this shows you the false confidence that alcohol can give you, often at the most inappropriate moments! Not the cleverest decision in the history of the world, but hey, at least I'm still here to tell the tale.

By the end of our time in Melbourne then, despite all the good times, we were all rather cold, tired, and certainly in need of some sunshine. Next stop, Noosa!

"Summer, summer, summertime!"

Compared to the cooler temperatures of Melbourne, Noosa was a true sunny delight. Not only was this a surfing town with a laid back vibe, it turned out that the only accessible hotel that Jos had been able to find was a Sheraton, meaning that we got to live in relative luxury for the last week of our trip. Managing to pack three different climates into our adventure was an achievement too, but I was definitely glad we'd saved the warmest place for last, as it made surviving Melbourne even sweeter.

For the first time on our journey we got a hire car, as we were now a bit more out in the sticks and would need a more permanent mode of transport to get around. The guy who delivered the hire car to us was quite an eccentric character, and had driven a long way to bring it to us, so Jon ended up mimicking his mannerisms for the rest of the week, leaving us all in fits of giggles. As I was unable to drive anything but my own adapted car back in the UK, Emma and Jon split the driving between them, though we certainly didn't go on any excessive road trips.

With only a week left of our holiday and plenty packed in already, we soon tuned ourselves in to the relaxed surfer vibe in Noosa and spent plenty of time chilling on the beach, me with my top off (ooh matron!) enjoying the feeling of the sun warming my chest, a marked difference from the layers we were wrapped in while in Melbourne. We were even lucky enough to see a pod of dolphins swim past, which only added to the amazing tropical feeling. In fact, Noosa was where we finally got a taste of the outback and Australia's rich and abundant wildlife, in both natural and unnatural settings.

One of the first things we did was take a trip to Steve Irwin's zoo. Steve was still alive at this time, and I'd loved watching his wildlife shows back in Britain, so I was really keen to check out his project. At the zoo we saw koalas, kangaroos and even some Tasmanian Devils. Although it was a great place to visit, I always find zoos a bit sad and I was really eager to see some of these animals in the wild if I possibly could.

Lucikly for me, one evening Jon and me took a walk out of Noosa, where the landscape very quickly became quite remote. Initially our walk was an accessible one, but soon we got to the point where there was a sign saying 'buggies and wheelchairs no further'. Being our usual daredevil selves (hey, I start fights with strangers remember!) we decided to ignore this sign and carried on regardless. The pathway though got gradually rockier and rockier, to the point where we were actually forced to turn back whether we liked it or not. In those extra ten minutes of off-piste adventure though, suddenly everyone we ran into, no doubt aware of the big sign that we'd flatly ignored, were suddenly all smiles and conversation. It was all "hey, great to see you out!" whereas before we'd had trouble getting a word out of anyone we'd met on the street. It was really good that people were finally opening up to us a bit, spurred on by my refusal to be stopped by road safety signs, and even more fantastically, by going that extra ten minutes down the road we got to see koalas in the wild as well, proof that sometimes it is good to break the rules!

A few nights later, walking back from a bar, more than a little tipsy and with Jon on the back of the chair, we cruised over the boardwalks, through the pine trees and listened to the crickets singing in the warm night air. Like I said before, it is often the smaller moments that stick with you, and experiencing the beautiful wildlife of Australia really quenched my thirst for travel, adventure, and new points of view.

If I had to pick out any low points from our final week in Oz though, it would have to be our daytrip to Brisbane, which was about an hours drive away from Noosa. Although I am sure there any many good points about Brisbane and I'm aware that we only got a brief glimpse of it on an overwhelmingly grey day, I really wasn't keen on it as a city, especially when compared to Sydney and Melbourne. With its grey concrete and very tall skyscrapers, it just didn't feel like it had much character to it, so I was glad we hadn't chosen it as a base for our third week.

Back in Noosa though, we watched England play Australia in the Ashes, which, in 2005, were being held in England. It was a great experience to be in Australia and watching England win the series for the first time since 1987, although I made sure not to be too vocal about my happiness in case I got in trouble with the locals!

Before we knew it though, the week and our holiday were sadly drawing to a close and it was time to get back to Blighty. The eccentric guy who had brought the hire car all that way for us now met us at the airport in Brisbane in order to pick it up again, and it was time for us to wave goodbye to Australia and board the plane to Singapore.

"One tequila, two tequila, three tequila, floor"

In Singapore the first time round, Jon had bumped into an old friend from his uni days and arranged to meet her for a drink on the return leg. Emma and me were happy to hang out on our own, especially as we were both quite tired after the long haul flight. As before, we didn't have a hoist in our hotel because we were only staying one night, so the plan was for Emma and Jon to transfer me again. By the time Jon got back to the hotel though, much later than expected, and certainly a lot drunker, it was clear that Emma was going to have to transfer me herself. This wasn't exactly ideal and was a bit of a hairy experience for me, but we managed to get there in the end. Once we were all safely tucked up in bed, we all still managed to get a decent bit of shuteye before our flight home in the morning.

The flight home went as smoothly as one could hope, but it was one of mixed feelings for me. While I was sad that my first solo adventure had come to an end, I was also looking forward to getting home, sleeping in my own bed (remember, I'd been top and tailing with Jon for three weeks now) and having some home cooked meals again. Though I was too close to the experience to be able to analyse it all properly, I was already very proud of what I'd managed to achieve on this journey, despite and indeed because of all the ups and downs that we'd been through together. I was also looking forward to seeing my family again. Even though I'd been on the phone to them, especially my Mum, during my time in Oz, I knew my Mum wasn't going to be happy until she saw me in the flesh and had the chance to feed me a good home cooked meal, something I was more than happy to let her do!

So what had I learnt from my first solo adventure to the other side of the world? Well, a lot of things. Many of these lessons took a while to sink in though, and I wasn't initially aware of the value of what I'd learnt. Though I certainly learnt a lot about PA relationships and budgets, over the next few years I definitely made some of the same mistakes again. In the end then, the lessons that I really hung on to from my first major trip, were that I was madly and deeply in love with travel and wanted to start planning my next holiday as soon as I possibly could. And the other major lesson? People will always be people, and no matter how hard you try and keep things under control, they will always surprise you, sometimes for the worst, but most of the time for the best.

Chapter Three – America

"American Boy"

I first ventured "across the pond" in 1987, at the tender age of four, to meet Mickey Mouse and his friends at Disney World, Florida. Obviously this wasn't a solo adventure, but with my family's support, I learnt to swim for the first time, something that has remained important to me ever since. Due to my condition, there are not many sports that I can participate in, or exercises that are suitable for me – I'm never going to be a champion weightlifter for example – but swimming is something I've been able to enjoy ever since, which made learning at such a young age a liberating experience. It has also been something I've made the most of throughout my life, which you'll be reading more about later in this chapter.

My other main memory of this first trip to The States isn't quite so pleasant, and involves a certain world famous mouse, that lives in a certain so called "Magic Kingdom". As I'd started using my first electric wheelchair at the age of 3 – I'll leave you to imagine the joys of teaching a 3 year old to steer accurately – when we got to Disney World, I was unable to climb the stairs to reach Mickey, a problem I share in common with those other famous characters, the Daleks. So in the end, Mickey had to come down to see me. Unfortunately for Mickey and my poor parents I wasn't excited by this prospect at all, in fact I was terrified! For some reason I'd got it into my head that Mickey had mistaken me for a block of cheese, and was actually coming down the stairs to eat me! Imagine the horror of watching a larger-than-life mouse moving towards you, all the time waving and doing a jaunty dance, if you thought he was going to eat you, absolute nightmare! Cue an hysterical crying fit, my family trying to console me, and poor Mickey trying to convince me that he was in fact a very friendly mouse and had absolutely no interest in putting me on top of a cracker and having me for lunch. Let's just say I took a lot of convincing.

Thankfully for my parents, I must've got over my phobia of Mickey Mouse, because I was able to return to Florida and Disney World as a teenager, this time with Mum, my Stepdad Dave, Claire Bear, and my stepbrothers Robbie and Jamie. This experience was a much more positive one, and although I was quite poorly after a major back operation, and so unable to go on most of the rides, I was at least able to cruise around sunny Florida with my stepbrothers, listening to Nelly and thinking we were the coolest kids in town – ahh the Noughties.

In between these two trips to the Sunshine State, I'd also travelled to Washington and New York with my Dad, to meet up with his old school friend. As I was very young then too, my memories of this trip are mainly based on viewing the camera footage of it so many times. Dad's friend will pop up again in a later chapter though, so my first trip is worth mentioning, no matter how little of it I remember. There certainly weren't any mice involved though, I made sure of that.

"Mexican or Mexican't?"

This chapter isn't just about North America though; it's also about Central America, specifically Mexico, which is where I went for my next family adventure in April 2010. I know I was in the safe cocoon of my family again, including Mum, Dave and Claire, but going to Mexico as a disabled person in a wheelchair felt like taking a leap into the unknown. Although Mum had done a lot of research and decided that it was a safe place for me to visit, as with any trip to a new country, I was quite nervous about how the journey would go, especially as in this case it would involve an 11 hour flight, on a par with Singapore and Australia. Despite the nerves though, I was also really excited to be visiting a new country. The months leading up to our trip had proved quite stressful for me. I'd been really ill with a chest infection and had been chasing all over the place trying to get my car fixed and my life in order, in preparation for starting my newly promoted job at Scope, which was due to begin shortly after our holiday.

Getting away from it all and having some time to chill out and relax was certainly something I was looking forward to then, and an all-inclusive holiday at a luxurious resort in sunny Mexico sounded like just the ticket. Although the flight was long, the journey from Gatwick, complete with all my transfers in and out of the plane, went as smoothly as I could've wanted. Though my legs stiffened up a lot on the flight, and subsequently were killing me by the time we arrived, it was nothing a good nights sleep wouldn't fix. On top of aching legs though, I also had a mild chest infection that I was worried was going to get worse if I wasn't careful. In the end, I decided to start taking the antibiotics that I'd brought with me, though this meant I wouldn't be able to indulge in the free drinks that came with our all-inclusive package, but hey, you can't drink them all, no matter how much I would've liked to try! At times like this, despite it affecting the amount of fun I might be able to have, I really have to put my health first, as I know the consequences of ignoring a chest infection can be dire, especially after being hospitalised with pneumonia in the past.

I took the first few days of the holiday slowly as a result of my chest, and spent most of my time chilling by the pool, soaking up as many rays as possible. This definitely proved to be the best medicine, and within three days I was feeling much perkier and ready to be a bit more active.

The hotel was by far the biggest and most luxurious I'd been lucky enough to stay in. Surrounded by swaying palms, and leading down to a shimmering white sand beach, the grounds of the hotel were more stunning than the interior, and the sun certainly did me the world of good. After those initial days of resting up, I started swimming in the pool every day and even decided to take the plunge and try out some SCUBA diving in the pool too. Although it was a strange feeling, knowing that I could pull the hand of Mum and Lisa (my parents next door neighbour since I was 4, who had come along on the holiday with her daughter Kirsty, and her friend Dale) if I felt uncomfortable meant that I began to relax into it after the first few minutes and ultimately really enjoyed the experience.

I left the water thinking that I'd love to do it in the open sea one day, which goes to show that while I always enjoy an experience, I'm always wondering whether I can take it to the next level. While this might all sound a bit reckless and daredevilish, I only do these things because I have built up to them slowly and I really trust the people that I have around me. Without that trust, I wouldn't dare put my head under water for any length of time! It is all about knowing your limits after all, but also being aware of which ones you are capable of stretching just that little bit further...

As it turned out, this was just the beginning of my watery adventures in Mexico, as on the Wednesday, about half way through the trip, we travelled out to a special diving school where I was going to have the opportunity to swim with dolphins! This was a lifetime ambition for me, dolphins really are amazing creatures and I'd always wanted to be in the water with them, especially after watching so many David Attenborough documentaries as a child. Leaving the hotel had proved tricky due to the lack of accessible transport and accessible places to visit. Taking me to swim with dolphins ended up being the only time we left the resort, and as the diving school was 40 minutes drive away, we sourced the same taxi that had picked us up from the airport.

Sadly for us, there had been torrential rain all morning, so when we arrived at the school, there was some doubt as to whether I would be able to do it or not. Even if the rain did stop, the ground was soaking and there were huge puddles everywhere, which my wheelchair would have difficulty navigating. We decided to sit out the storm in a bar, and luckily for me Tottenham were playing Arsenal in the North London Derby and this was the year that Danny Rose scored the winning wonder goal for Spurs, meaning that for once we got to beat our arch rivals! Getting to see this goal almost made me thankful for the rain, but unfortunately by this time I had missed by 45-minute slot. My Mum though, always excellent at a charm offensive and a bit of negotiation, managed to persuade the guys to let me have a 10 minute go after the storm had passed. Although we weren't in the open sea, it was still a large body of water, but just seeing the dolphins erased all of my fears. Once I was in the water, the dolphins were at first a bit hesitant to come close. My knees don't straighten properly, and it almost felt like they were aware of my physical vulnerability and therefore felt cautious and didn't want to hurt me.

When I turned to the side though, I was able to get closer to them and eventually I managed to stroke them and give them a kiss. This really was an amazing experience, they are such gentle and beautiful animals and being in such close proximity to them, it is easy to see why they are believed to be one of the most intelligent species on this planet.

As the week drew to a close and we were coming to the end of our season in the sun, the unexpected happened. On the other side of the world, a volcano erupted and suddenly we were stranded. The Icelandic ash cloud, caused by the eruption of Eyjafjallajökull (kudos if you know how to pronounce that!) caused worldwide disruption in April 2010 when it covered a vast swathe of Europe, which led to a large number of flights being cancelled altogether. Although there are worse places to be stuck than a luxury resort in sunny Mexico, the situation did cause some problems for us all. As the hotel was a classy resort, Thompson, the travel company we had booked the holiday with, wanted to bump us to a less pricey hotel down the road for the extra days we were due to be staying. Luckily for me though, being disabled was actually going to be an advantage for once, as the less luxurious hotel wasn't accessible and so I couldn't be moved. So while half of our party had to decamp to a Travelodge style affair, me, Mum and Dave got to stay in the relative luxury of the resort for a few more days. The weather also improved after the rain we'd had midweek, and by this time I was off the antibiotics so I was finally able to indulge in a few drinks. Thank you Eyjafjallajökull!

After 4 nights though, the cracks were beginning to show. Not only were we worried we were going to have to start paying for some of this, we were also concerned we were going to be flown to Madrid and then left to make our own way home. With my first day in the new job at Scope fast approaching as well, I was now starting to feel the stress and was very keen to get back to life, back to reality.

Once we were safely back in blighty though (thankfully without having to go via Madrid) I was able to reflect on the trip as a whole, and realise that it was one of the best holidays I'd ever been on. Not only had I stayed at an amazing resort, I'd got to swim nearly every day. I'd fulfilled a lifetime ambition by swimming with dolphins, and I'd got to spend the entire trip with some amazing family members and friends, and particularly my sister Claire, who had recently turned 21. Cancun is definitely a place I would recommend to other disabled travellers, and although we didn't leave the resort that much due to the inaccessibility of some parts of the area, the resort and the places we researched which were accessible, were all very accommodating and met and exceeded all of our needs. It was also fantastic to realise that I could travel to places that I hadn't necessarily thought were possible for someone in a wheelchair, preconceptions are there to be challenged after all, and travelling to Mexico was the perfect example of that.

"California Dreamin'"

My next journey across the Atlantic came a few years later, in 2011. At this time I was still working at Scope, and though I now had the financial means to go on an epic holiday due to my regular work, I didn't have as much free time as I once did. As a result, planning the trip and making the best use of our time was even more important this time around than it had been for Australia seven years earlier.

Back in our pre-Disability Horizons days, my friend Srin Madipalli had just finished training to be a lawyer and had decided to take some time out for a bit of travelling and adventure before he started practising the law. During this time he travelled to Thailand, Bali and

South Africa with his PA's in tow, and he was now planning to go on to Boston, Massachusetts, to meet up with some friends. A few months before he'd left, we'd discussed the idea of my joining him for the South African leg of his tour, but in the end it had proved too expensive for me to fly out and join him, but we agreed we should go on holiday somewhere else in the future.

A few of the places we considered were Brazil and Cuba, but sadly for us there seemed to be no accessible vehicles in Cuba at that time, and though Brazil seemed more doable, we were running out of time to do the necessary research. Also, although Brazil has come on in leaps and bounds, we still believed we would run into many more accessibility issues than we would in the USA. We'd also both been to America before, and so we were both comfortable and confident that we wouldn't run into any major issues there. As I'd been to New York, Florida and DC before, I wasn't keen to go to any of those places again, but I still hadn't explored the West Coast, and the thought of going to the home of some of my favourite Hip Hop artists proved too good an opportunity to miss!

In the end then, we decided we'd meet up in San Francisco, a city I'd never been to before and was longing to see. The plan was to start our road trip there, before driving out into the desert to visit Las Vegas, and then heading back into California to LA. We knew there would be a lot of driving involved and a lot of time on the road, but spending time driving in America is a very different beast to driving in the UK, and the lure of driving through the desert like some sort of wheelchair cowboy was too good to resist!

Though we both knew San Fran had a reputation for being quite hilly, we decided to take the plunge anyway, deciding that if we had to charge our batteries more regularly then so be it, we'd still be charging them in San Francisco! After weeks of organising the logistics, we decided that Srin would fly from Boston with his PA Hugh, pick up the hire car that was big enough for all of us, and then Tina and me would fly from Heathrow and they'd meet us at the airport at the other end. Tina was an ex girlfriend but really a lifelong friend from my uni days. She came back from Austria to support me on the trip, within very much the same arrangement as Emma and Jon. She was paid as my carer, she spent her income on the costs, and everyone was happy.

Next came the not so small task of packing. Packing is a bit of a stressful activity for everyone, but when you're disabled, packing the essentials often means bringing sizeable items of equipment with you, items that you wouldn't be able to keep clean or get into bed without. Although I have often arranged to hire a hoist before jetting off on holiday, luckily for me, Srin had decided to bring his mo-lift hoist and his shower chair with him, and we would be able to share. Usually on holiday I can manage on bed baths alone, but as this was going to be a longer trip and in hopefully warmer temperatures at times, I was very thankful for the shower chair — nothing worse than being stuck in a car for hours on end with a smelly person after all! Thankfully, with other essentials such as my sling for the hoist, the chair charger and my knee pad to prevent me getting pressure sores on my knees at night, I just managed to keep within the baggage weight limit and we were ready to go! If disability related stuff does take you over the check-in limit though, explain that you are travelling with essential disability equipment and they should make allowances for you.

Although all airlines are obligated to cater for wheelchair users, some are definitely better at it than others, so if the prices for the bigger airlines aren't too out of reach, then it always feels like they are safer bets when it comes to service. With this in mind, we decided to fly out with BA as it was a decent price for such a long haul flight, and it was direct. Unlike with Australia, we were more relaxed this time about not booking every single thing in advance. As we'd both visited America before and knew that it was excellent for accessibility, we felt we could risk booking some of the hotels when we actually got there, though we did book the San Fran hotel in advance and decided to stay at the Crowne Plaza San Fran Airport Hotel. Although it was quite a generic and chainy hotel, it met all of our needs, was fully accessible and we were able to get accessible rooms (plus an accessible shuttle bus to and from the hotel to the centre of San Francisco was available).

With America being the gas guzzling country that it is, we knew we'd need the freedom of having a hire car. After doing some googling around for the cheapest option, we found a company that would have the car delivered to San Fran and then let us leave it at LAX Airport when we eventually flew home. Unfortunately, the car door jammed on day two of our San Fran stint, but the hire company were fantastic and came out immediately to give us a replacement vehicle. Eventually, it turned out that this one had some issues too, so they gave us a third and final car shortly before our planned drive out to Vegas. Clearly none of this was ideal, but the hire company made sure that we had the correct wheels in the end, and the car was big enough for all of us, with both Tina and Hugh insured to drive, while Srin and me chilled with tunes.

Before we arrived in San Fran, Tina had not met Srin or Hugh, and although I obviously knew Srin, we hadn't spent much solid time together, and I didn't know Hugh at all. I was a little apprehensive about whether we would get on therefore, but being the chilled, laid back and generally cool people that we are, we all clicked immediately. On the first night we took a trip into central San Fran and went to a very hip Organic restaurant for our first taste of Californian cuisine. As I've said before, my picky eating habits have caused problems in the past, particularly when it comes to experiencing new cultures and cuisines, but in America I felt right at home as their cuisine is pretty similar to ours. After our first taste of the city, Tina and me didn't last much longer and we'd made it to bed by 9pm, both exhausted after our near 24-hour journey.

The next day though, rested and revived, we were ready to go exploring and experience all that San Francisco had to offer, and boy was this a lot! From the very beginning I loved the laid back and alternative vibe that the city gave off, it seemed so much more chilled than the other cities I had visited on the East Coast. Before leaving the UK, I'd been much more excited about visiting LA and getting to see the places where all my favourite West Coast Hip Hop stars hung out, but San Francisco truly took me by surprise with its hipness and its friendly and alternative vibe.

On that first day, despite the already documented car issues, we managed to take an accessible boat ride around San Francisco Bay, from which we saw the spectacular Golden Gate Bridge and the notorious Alcatraz prison. Although we didn't stop off at Alcatraz, just seeing it from a distance sent chills down my spine, and seeing so many iconic sights meant that I had goosebumps pretty much all day. We also got our first proper glimpse of the Pacific Ocean from Golden Gate Park and generally had fun walking and rolling around the city. After just one day exploring, all my London-based stress had melted away and I was fully relaxed, with not a worry about work or health in sight. Screw the antibiotics I thought, from now on I'm going to prescribe myself some travel.

The next day was Sunday, and it was time to get out of the city and see some of those famous, epic American landscapes, which on this occasion meant Yosemite National Park. Tina was particularly excited about this trip, as she's a keen climber and had heard a lot about the mountainous landscapes. As we were there in November though, this meant snow, lots of snow, and after admiring the initial views from outside the park, we weren't sure what to do. We weren't actually allowed to enter unless we bought snow chains, so should we suck it up, be brave and buy them, or was it simply too risky for us to get stranded? After a quick chat, we agreed that this was a once-in-a-lifetime opportunity, and decided to take the plunge, pooled some money together and bought some snow chains for $75! Thankfully, Tina knew how to attach them, as us three Brits, unused to "proper" snow, didn't have the foggiest. Once they were attached, we drove carefully into the park through the slowly falling snowflakes and let the stunning views do the talking. There really is no view in Britain that can prepare you for the enormity of American landscapes. We saw the sheer rock face of El Capitain, surrounded by stark, frozen pines and saw tumbling waterfalls rushing into the icy pools of water below. As we drove around, with the heating on full blast, we were all in total awe of the glittering landscapes, and so glad we'd decided to take the plunge, agreeing that it was the best $75 we'd ever spent. Normally, I absolutely hate snow, as for me it means not being able to go outside and the frozen cold brings with it the threat of chest infections and a long winter of illness ahead, but in this foreign land, the snow took on a romantic, fairy tale quality and I couldn't get enough of it. Being in a car with snow chains and the heating on full blast helped me to appreciate it most of all of course!

We stopped off at a café on the way back to the hotel, and a sweet American waitress asked us in all seriousness whether "London was a big city in England?" which made us realise how much American culture has influenced us Brits, in comparison to how little, literally, they think of us! But then perhaps, with so much land and space, they think that anywhere the size of the UK must only have tiny little cities to its name.

On Monday, our final day in San Fran, we spent some more time cruising around the city, going to shops and cafes and soaking up the general laid-back atmosphere. After seeing the Golden Gate Bridge from various different viewing points around the city, we finally took a walk out onto it and posed for many photos, as who can resist such an iconic snapshot? In the evening, we were lucky enough to be taken out to dinner by my dad's old school friend, who got a mention at the start of the chapter when me and dad went to visit him in Washington DC. Since those days, he'd moved out West and treated us all to a fantastic meal at a Japanese restaurant called Benihana, where the chefs cut up, cook and juggle the food in front of you, it was definitely a great end to our time in San Fran.

On the whole, San Fran had proved itself to be a very accessible city and although having the hire car meant that we could drive out to places like Yosemite, I think we would've managed to navigate the city centre without it, as the transport was accessible, most of the buildings were too and the people were very friendly, warm and open. The friendly and open atmosphere in San Fran is one that has really stuck with me ever since, and I found it to be the embodiment of the sort of liberal, chilled and warm vibe that I really love. I'd really like to go back again some day, and it was certainly a fantastic start to our American road trip.

"What happens in Vegas..."

The next morning, sparkly eyed and freshly showered (or should that be a bit tired and hungover...) I was ready to embark on what would prove to be the longest road trip of my life, up until this point anyway. Although an estimated 10 hours on the road sounded daunting, driving through the desert with the radio on proved to be much more enjoyable that I thought it would be. Nothing can prepare you for the vast and almost alien landscape that is the Nevada desert, and it was easy to lose hours of the drive by just staring out of the window in awe. This was certainly a different view than the ones you got back home in England, not a sheep in sight for one thing! Being with good friends also helped the time to pass, and thankfully I'd invested in a Kindle before setting off for the States (reasonably new technology back in 2010 don't you know!) so I had something else to keep me entertained, as I didn't have to focus on driving. By the time we approached Vegas itself, night had fallen and it was truly one of the oddest experiences, after driving through empty desert for hours, to suddenly see this mass of neon lights ahead of us. The city seemed to appear out of nowhere, and it gave me goosebumps once again to see this iconic, supposedly sinful city rising out of the desert before us.

My initial reaction to Vegas was nothing but positive, and I couldn't wait to get stuck in. The lights were bright, joyous and a little overwhelming, and everything was exactly how you expected it to be. We'd booked our rooms in advance when we were back in the UK, as Vegas is such a popular destination and tends to get booked up very quickly. We'd decided to go with one of the biggest resorts on the strip, the MGM Grand, and "Grand" almost seemed like an understatement. The complex had two enormous theatres, a massive casino, loads of shops and a lot of restaurants, not to mention the hundreds of hotel rooms on offer. Unfortunately though, despite all this grandeur, we hit our first set of accessibility hitches upon arrival at the hotel. Firstly, the valet parking had a bit of an issue with our side ramps, but this was just a simple matter of teaching people new tricks, and so we soon had them sorted. The bigger problem for us both though, was that the showers in our supposedly accessible rooms both had steps, so not so accessible after all. Being a lawyer,

Srin was a great person to have on side, as in the past I might have shied away from kicking up a fuss. This though, was a matter of principle and it is essential that you do 'kick up a fuss' in such a situation, not only to educate people but also to tackle unfair discrimination. Srin and me headed back down to reception to explain and they couldn't have been more helpful about it. American customer service is generally way ahead of the game and they put Srin and Hugh in a different, and this time fully accessible room, and then much to our delight, bumped me and Tina up to a "Celebrity Spa room" as there were no other standard accessible rooms left. Once again, being disabled was finally paying off! The room was the height of luxury, with a very nice roll-in shower and a lot of space to move around in. After unpacking and settling in to our newfound celebrity status, we were all eager to go for a look around the hotel and get our first taste of the rock 'n' roll Vegas lifestyle.

Nothing prepares you for the sheer scale of Vegas. It really is a vast, glittering money-making machine, with every last square foot perfectly designed to try and get cash out of you. From the endless rows of one-armed-bandits, to the 24 hour all-you-can-eat buffets, while the glamour dazzles you at first, you quickly come to realise there is something quite depressing about it all. With no windows or clocks in any of the casinos so that you lose all track of time, and blank faced people mechanically putting dollars into slot machines, you soon realise that the dream that is being sold actually rings hollow, and the only people benefitting from this are the ones who own the casinos. The thing with Vegas though, is to realise this, shrug, and then get on with having fun anyway, and after a good nights rest in our luxurious suite, that is exactly what we set out to do.

Although it wasn't snowing here like in Yosemite, it was still freezing cold November weather. Thankfully though, most of the things to do in Vegas are inside, so we explored the Strip and all the hotels and casinos that it had to offer, which was quite frankly, an overwhelming amount. In order to get around, we used the totally accessible monorail, which given the inclement weather (very cold by Vegas standards, apparently we brought the UK weather with us) was the warmest available option. Highlights of the day included seeing the Gondolas and the replica of Venice inside the grand Venetian hotel, and after admiring the view from the very top of the Stratosphere Hotel, watching Hugh do a Base Jump off of it (twice!) which was both thrilling and stomach churning in equal measure! After a bit more exploring, we hit up the bar, but with Tina on a detox, and us not being in a big drinking mood, it wasn't exactly like a scene from *The Hangover.* I think if I'd gone to Vegas with a hard drinking bunch of people, like with my stepbrothers Robbie and Jamie (not that I'm implying anything guys…) then I might have got into the spirit of Vegas a bit more, that spirit being, the drunker you are, the more you'll probably enjoy it – up to a point anyway. As things were though, after some not very impressive food at one of the all-you-can-eat buffets, we headed back to our rooms after a hard days sightseeing, ready to roll into bed.

We had a lot planned for our second (and final) day in Vegas, and this began with leaving it behind entirely and heading out to visit the Hoover Dam and Lake Meade, which was an hour's drive away. Designed to tame the mighty Colorado River, the dam was completed in 1935 and is a truly spectacular sight for sore eyes. After soaking up the history and the things the human race can achieve when we put our minds to it, we drove back to Vegas in time to watch Cirque de Soleil. This was a fantastic show, jam-packed with death-defying acrobatics, mystery, dance and beautiful imagery. I completely lost all sense of time while watching it, and this wasn't just because there were no clocks like in the casinos. It really was a magical show, and if you're ever in Vegas, I recommend you take the time to go and see them. After an hour and a half of culture though, it was time to get down to the real business of Las Vegas, gambling! Having spent most of my money getting to America in the first place, I didn't have that much to waste (and waste really is the essence of gambling) but with what I had, I hit up the Texas hold 'em poker, and it turns out after years of playing it at Coventry, I was…shit. I won the first hand, but I then made the school boy error of getting cocky about it and lost it all again in the blink of an eye. Sigh. Srin had a go at the roulette table and wasn't any more successful than me, and we all had a few goes on the slot machines, though these weren't exactly the most exciting way to gamble. As I didn't have much money to begin with, the gambling part of the holiday was over pretty quickly, and if I were ever to go back, I'd definitely take a set amount of cash with me that I knew it would be fine to squander away, when in Vegas after all…

For some of us though, the wild thrills and Hangover style shenanigans weren't over yet. Interestingly, we did actually find one of the apartment buildings we think was featured in *The Hangover* and took a video of ourselves outside it. For Srin, Tina and me though, some gambling was as wild as it got (we certainly didn't take mushrooms during Cirque de Soleil) but for Hugh, the night had only just begun…Being a big boxing fan, and aware that the MGM Grand was known for hosting big boxing matches, Hugh asked Srin if after he helped him to bed, he could go and have a wind down drink and watch the match. Hours later, Srin was uncomfortable in bed and wanted to turn over, something he needed Hugh's help for. Unable to get in contact with him, there was nothing he could do but lay there and wait. Meanwhile, it transpired that Hugh had indulged in more than a few drinks and had got himself well and truly smashed, only to get into a boxing match of his own! To be fair to Hugh, the other guy swung at him first, but in an act of self-defence, Hugh landed a punch too, which brought the casino's security swooping down and ushering Hugh into a little room where he was made to explain the events in front of CCTV footage. The only reason he managed to escape the security guards unpunished, and avoided getting chucked out of the hotel altogether, was that he explained that he was Srin's PA and that he needed to get back to him. He returned to a now very uncomfortable and annoyed Srin four hours after setting out, looking rather sheepish and had to explain the night's events.

The next morning then, after informing us of Hugh's exploits, which thankfully we'd been blissfully unaware of, the atmosphere on the road to LA was a little tense to say the least. Tina had to do the bulk of the driving as Hugh was feeling a little 'delicate' and Srin was quite rightly in a bad mood as this wasn't exactly good PA behaviour. All's well that ends well though, and the further we drove, the better everyone felt, though it was another long journey, this time four hours, to LA.

I was surprised that I hadn't enjoyed Vegas as much as I thought I would. Though I didn't regret going there, and it was great to see all the lights, glitz and glamour, I found the whole experience more of a downer than I had expected. Seeing so many people mindlessly gambling their lives away in sweat pants took the edge off. It certainly wasn't all romance and jazz like in Sinatra's time, and the lack of natural light in the casinos, coupled with the generally rubbish food, made the whole place feel a bit claustrophobic. It did get a big thumbs up on the accessibility front though, which is always good news. Perhaps if I'd been there in the sizzling heat of summer I might've got a better impression of the place, but as it was I was glad we were heading to LA for some warmer weather, Hip Hop, and beach side living.

"California Loooooove!"

Compared to the epic 10-hour journey we'd had on route to Vegas, the four hours to LA flew by. Our hotel, the Best Western, was a bit generic and chainy but supposedly accessible, and was located near to LAX airport, which would hopefully cut down on any airport related stress when it was time for us to leave. We'd booked the hotel through Hotels.com when we were in San Fran, but upon arrival we hit the same problem we'd had in Vegas; the showers weren't roll in. The receptionist blamed Hotels.com for the mistake and told us there was nothing she could do about it, advising us to contact Hotels.com to resolve the issue. As there were only four days left of our trip, Srin and me agreed that bed baths would suffice and that they'd be less of a hassle than trying to find another hotel. When Srin got back to blighty he complained to Hotels.com and got a voucher for his troubles, so at least someone was willing to admit they were at fault.

After our usual unpacking and settling in session, we all convened outside to take in a new and alien concept on our holiday thus far...sun and warmth! This was a definite relief after the chilly temperatures in Las Vegas and we were amazed by the climate difference after just four hours drive, you certainly wouldn't get the equivalent temperature difference if you drove from London to Manchester! A taste of sunshine was especially welcome as I'd been so ill before the trip, and even more so as I knew winter was in full swing back in England.

As we were all a bit tired after the early morning and the relatively long drive, we decided the best thing to do with our weary bones was to take them to the beach for a spot of sunbathing. Growing up with so many American films, TV shows and music, Venice Beach is stamped into my mind as one of the coolest places on earth, and chilling on the beach in just a t-shirt felt like heaven after the claustrophobic atmosphere of Vegas. For the rest of the evening we cruised around the streets, checking out the Hollywood Hills, Beverly Hills and Sunset Boulevard, yet more names that mean so much to anyone who grew up on a diet of American culture. After a nice meal and a few drinks, we decided to call it a night reasonably early so we could wake up refreshed the next day and get on with some serious sightseeing.

On our first full day in LA, we did the typical American thing and spent most of it chilling on Malibu Beach and wandering aimlessly up and down Santa Monica Boulevard. I spent most of the time absorbing some much-needed vitamin D and admiring the view (and I do mean the view, not the suntanned American ladies!) Knowing we were in the home of Baywatch did add a certain glamour to the occasion though and I did half expect to see Pamela Anderson appear out of the water, but sadly we had no such luck!

On the following day we decided to take a drive up the famous Pacific route 1, which goes all the way up into Canada, although obviously we didn't intend to drive that far. The views as we drove up the coast were absolutely stunning and left us all feeling very inspired. After stopping off for lunch, we drove down Hollywood Boulevard with the intention of getting out and seeing the famous Walk of Fame, but sadly we couldn't get out as there was a huge crowd gathered to watch the Christmas lights being turned on. Instead, we went and visited the Hollywood sign-viewing platform at the Griffiths Observatory, so we could all get our Hollywood Hills photos (and video blogs) under our belts. As everyone always says, the classic Hollywood sign does look a lot smaller and dare I say it, tackier, in real life, as did much of LA. Hollywood Boulevard itself looked very run down and extremely tacky and all of the famous neighbourhoods like Beverley Hills just seemed highly pretentious.

As with most things, the glitz and the glamour that you see on TV isn't as evident in reality, or perhaps I'm just getting old and cynical.

The next day we set out to discover the humble abode of the man who became the prince of a town called Bel-Air…Growing up, *The Fresh Prince of Bel-Air* was one of my favourite shows, so I was desperate to track down the house where the Banks family lived and sing the song outside it, as I'm sure many thousands of others have done before me. We drove around Rodeo Drive, Beverly Hills and Bel Air, before rocking up to the "Banks Residence", as Geoffrey so haughtily described it. This was a really fun pop-culture moment for all of us, and it had much more of an impact on me than seeing the Hollywood sign. After that, I fancied going for a cocktail on Sunset Boulevard, but after driving for thirty minutes, we realised we were driving away from the cocktail bars and as the sun disappeared over the horizon, we'd missed our magical cocktail moment.

Thankfully though, we made up for this mistake on the last night and got our cocktails on Sunset, followed by dinner by Manhattan Beach, one of my favourite areas of LA. It was in this neighbourhood that we found a classic American sports bar, with memorabilia on the walls and a pool table, where I showed Srin how I played pool from my chair. We also had a fantastic meal at an Italian restaurant in this area and found all the locals to be very welcoming and friendly. The majority of bars and restaurants were fully accessible, and all of the ones we went to had accessible restrooms.

Aside from the *Fresh Prince of Bel-Air* pilgrimage, there was one other pop-culture place I wanted to visit that held a very special place in my heart. Although this might be a bit cringey to admit to now, as a young teenager I was a complete wannabe gangster. The first album I bought, with my thumb placed securely over the 'Parental Advisory' sticker, was Warren G, *Regulate,* so with West

Coast rappers like Snoop Dogg and Dre held up as such icons in my teenage mind, I was desperate to visit the neighbourhoods that had inspired the music, namely Compton, Long Beach and Inglewood. To get our pilgrimage off on the right track, we tuned in to KDAY 935 radio, which played a lot of West Coast hip hop and rap. Srin couldn't believe I also knew all the lyrics, but like I said, I really was dedicated to becoming a gangster back in the leafy, sleepy village of St Ives. Being the silly, easily led chaps that we are, we'd got it into our heads that we were going to be driving into a bullet ridden neighbourhood, with firebombs going off left, right and centre. Living in Hackney at the time, another area with a bad reputation but funnily enough no firebombs, I should've known better than to go looking for cheap thrills, but if LA taught me anything, it's that the gap between fantasy and reality is a very large one and it's easy to fall into.

"From celebrity central, to cold, snowy England"

On the last day, after doing a bit of souvenir shopping, we soaked up the final rays of the LA sun and tried to prepare ourselves mentally for returning to snowy and icy Britain, something I certainly wasn't looking forward to. When we got to the airport we found out our flight was delayed by two hours due to the ice and snow at home, which wasn't great. As per usual though, Srin and me, along with Tina and Hugh, were going to be the first to be put on the flight because we're wheelchair users and the airport staff need to get us down the central aisle and into our seats. In the departure lounge, while we were waiting to get lifted, and thinking of the long flight ahead, who should walk through the door to lift all our spirits but Jack Black! He was also going to be boarded early because of his VIP status and we got to sit with him in the departure lounge as we waited to be settled on board. I tried not to be starstruck, though he is one of my favourite actors, and we decided to strike up a conversation. He was a genuinely nice guy, I chatted to his companion as well who was also really cool, and then I decided to grab the bull by the horns and ask if he'd do a quick video blog for me to promote MartynSibley.com. Being the gentleman that he is he said he would, and then did four takes of it on my flipcam to make sure he perfected it. The resulting video is still on my website to this day and this encounter left me with a huge smile on my face and made the hassle of getting onto the plane seem a lot less stressful.

The flight itself was quite long and arduous and I felt uncomfortable for a lot of it, but the air steward commented on my snoring when we landed, so I must've got some sleep in the end. Landing back in 0 degree England after being awake for 24 hours was definitely a shock to the system and to add to our troubles, my car, which we'd left in the long stay car park, chose this moment not to start! Although by this point I was pretty close to losing it and panicking, thankfully the customer service staff were very helpful and provided us with somewhere warm to shelter while they jump started the car. When we finally got back to London I slept better than I had the entire trip and was very glad to be tucked up in my own bed.

All in all, my experiences of America have all been hugely positive. As a disabled person, I think it is one of the best places in the world for accessibility, and as American's pride themselves so much on the quality of their customer service, if something goes wrong they are generally desperate to put it right. There is still so much of the USA that I would love to see, and I intend to go back as soon as I can, and outside of the US, I'd also love to travel back to Mexico and even explore other countries in South America, as they are all likely to become more and more accessible over the coming years. Brazil in particular is a country that I would love to visit, so watch this space…When it comes to the USA and Mexico though, my advice as always, is to do your research, find out what will be the easiest way for you to travel around the country and invest your time and effort into uncovering the best accessible hotels you can get for your buck. Though as Srin and me found out, sometimes things won't be as described on the website, and if this is the case then always make sure to complain, because you are the one in the right and you deserve good service just as much as anyone else.

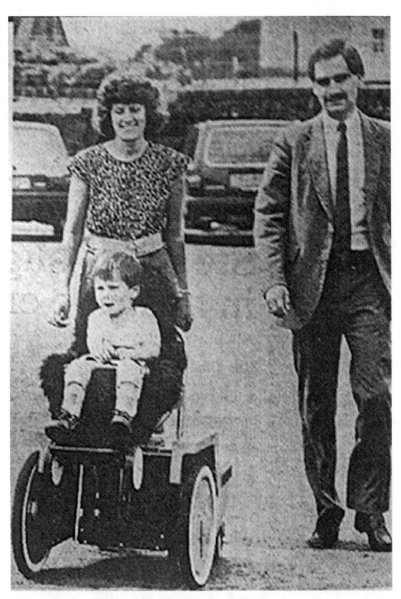

With my mum and dad aged 3 trying out my new wheels

Sibling cuddles with Claire

Hello tiger!

Rolling with Dave, Rob and Jamie

In 2005 at Sydney Harbour on my first voyage

Sharing amazing moments with Jon and Emma

Me and Srin on the Golden Gate bridge in San Francisco

A snowy Yosemite park and the snow-chain-crew
Srin, myself, Tina and Hugh

The wheely well travelled friends
Toby, Srin and yours truly

Biggest smile ever after flying over Stonehenge

Recording a piece to camera from a hot air balloon over Catalonia

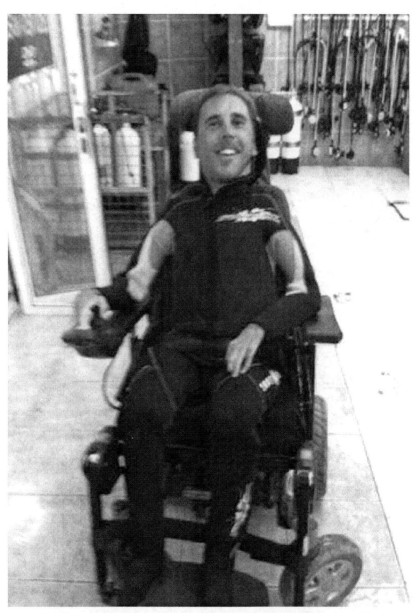

Most awkward and most amazing wetsuit in the world

Swing low sweet heavy chariot

Abseiling on "the edge of glory"

Skiing with the Train and Play team

*With my kochanie (Polish for sweetheart) Kasia
on our crazy adventure in Scotland*

High viz and high up

Did we pack everything guys

Highland sunset

Success at Lands End

European Voluntary Service volunteering in Asturias Espana

Getting all creative on the Aviles cider

*My amazing Lithuanian
grandfather
at Cambridge University*

*The brains and braun
from so many projects.
The fantastic Filipe Roldao*

Amsterdam on the Epic European Disability Roadtrip

*At the EEDR destination
of Vilnius Lithuania*

Wonderful Warsaw Poland

Precious Prague

Ferociously hot Barcelona

Lifes a beach in Catalonia

Montserrat and its stunning views

Sensational Sienna Italy

One of many beautiful people we met on the road.
Here is media guru Stefano

Perfect moments in Poland

A special easter Sunday with Kasia in Spain

At a Tokyo temple with Kasia and Haruka

Group photo with fellow delegates

Chilling with Mickey Mouse and less scared on this occasion

Me driving with my awesome adapted car

Adapted buses making tourism possible

Chapter Four – Adventure

Ever since I was a kid I've been keen to test my boundaries! Getting my first electric wheelchair at 3 years old and never feeling isolated because of my disability during my formative childhood years, meant that to a certain degree I've always been quite a confident and curious person, despite the nerves that I discussed in previous chapters. Overcoming those nerves though, has been part of the process, and being scared is something that I've tried to embrace as I've got older, as being worried or anxious is as much a part of life as feeling confident and care-free. One of the most important lessons I've learnt is not to feel anxious about being anxious – it is a natural feeling and it doesn't have to get in the way of what you want to achieve.

So while this chapter is in no way suggesting that all disabled people should go off and do crazy, adventurous things. I am suggesting that we all try and push our boundaries every once in a while. Whether that's learning to swim or starting a voluntary job. Not all attempts will be successful, and it's important to know your limits and accept what isn't possible – I'm never going to go into space for example, and bungee jumping is certainly out of the question! But I can do a lot of things, many of which I formerly thought were impossible, and though my own personal safety is always my number one priority, without facing up to a little bit of risk, human kind would never have achieved anything.

As I've mentioned in previous chapters, when it comes to any new experience, whether it's a holiday, a big move, or a spot of SCUBA diving, planning is everything. I really would like to stress how much planning and logistical thinking goes into everything I do, and how rigorously I research every hair-brained scheme that I have, in order to check it is safe, affordable and achievable. As I am clearly at more risk that most people when doing a physical activity, as I am unable to run away from danger or swim strongly, being in safe hands and working with well-respected and safety conscious companies is very important to me. If I didn't trust the people around me, then there is no way I would be taking to the sky or putting my head under water for any length of time, so researching companies before taking the plunge is essential for me.

With that in mind, I want to take you way back through the mists of time to August 2010…

Is it a bird? Is it a plane? It's Martyn Sibley!

Flying a plane in Salisbury

For as long as I can remember, I've wanted to fly a plane, and the fact that this has always been on my bucket list shows you what kind of kid I was. I didn't think it would be possible though until I started looking into it in the winter of 2009/2010 when I was laid up with a nasty chest infection and needed something to lift my mood. Planning for the future may not seem like the easiest thing to do when you're feeling rubbish, but it really helps to have something positive to aim for, especially if you know that thing is likely to take place in sunnier months when you're back on top form. My research, which involved watching videos of other disabled people flying, led me to the APT Charitable Trust in Salisbury, a charity that's dedicated to helping disabled people learn to fly. Based at Old Sarum Airfield, they have a small fleet of Microlight aircraft, all of which are two-seater, and one of which has specially adapted controls that can be used by disabled people with a range of different needs. It's possible to just go up for one journey or to train to be a fully qualified pilot with them, but as this was going to be my first attempt, I decided to pass on the pilot training for now!

By 2010 I'd already started working at Scope and had recently set up my blog, so this was the perfect opportunity to make a video to share with the world and show everyone exactly what disabled people are capable of! So, after a hard winter, August finally rolled around and my date with destiny in what looked like a very flimsy little plane, but I was assured it was one of the safest models ever, was finally here!

During the drive up from London, my nerves really started to kick in. Although I'd booked this date way in advance, it felt like it had snuck up on me all of a sudden and my adrenalin really started pumping as we got closer and closer to the airfield. When we arrived though, all thoughts of chickening out of the experience were put to one side once I met Raymond, my instructor and co-pilot for the day. His happy and enthusiastic nature made me feel like I was in safe hands, as did all the equipment they had in order to transfer me safely into the plane itself. A huge hoist on wheels went over the top of the plane, which allowed me to be lifted from my chair, straight into the aircraft. I was then strapped in and sat upright with the aid of Raymond and a lot of cushions. I was safely strapped in with a number of harnesses and my legs were strapped together so I'd be very secure once we got up in the air. I was positioned at the front of the plane, with a huge windscreen in front of me, giving me a panoramic view, while Raymond was in the seat behind. We were able to communicate via headsets and this made me feel a lot safer, as Raymond was able to talk me through everything that was happening.

Once we took off, it was one of the most exhilarating moments of my life to date. Although I hadn't realised, due to my rubbish geography, that we were so close to Stone Henge, that is exactly where we flew to within 20 minutes, and it was amazing to see such an iconic landmark from the air. Raymond let me take the controls for a little bit, and knowing that I was in charge was incredible. The reason I'd chosen to flay a plane was because I knew it would give me a huge buzz, but it would also be really very safe, whereas something like sky-diving would probably kill me. After all, this charity had be helping disabled people to fly for 10 years, I trusted that they knew what they were doing.

In the end, we were up in the sky for around 40 minutes, as you can see in the video, when we landed the smile on my face says it all. It is definitely something I'd love to do again one day, and if it's up your street and you are able, then it is something I'd highly recommend to other disabled people too. The guys at the charity really made me feel like I was in safe hands and there's nothing like seeing the earth from above to give you some perspective on life.

And for my next trick…

Is it a fish? Is it a shark? It's Martyn Sibley!

SCUBA Diving in Tenerife

In May 2012, a mobility equipment hire company called Lero invited me out to Tenerife to help promote their services. By this point in my career I'd left my job at Scope in order to pursue freelance work and broaden my horizons, and this was one of my first working holidays; Tenerife certainly wasn't a bad place to start. I ended up working with Lero for 12 months as a result of this trip, and ran their social media campaign, which helped me to feel secure in my new freelance role. I was there with Jon, who you'll remember from the Australia chapter, and we were both put up in the Mar Y Sol, an accessible hotel in Los Cristianos. With a pool out back and blazing hot sunshine, I was more than happy to be on a working trip, and with the carefree holiday spirit in my veins, I decided it was time to build on my SCUBA diving experience in Mexico and do a real dive in the sea!

After a test dive in the hotel swimming pool, we established a 'four pinch rule', meaning I would pinch the instructor four times if I wanted to come up for any reason. With this rule in place and the instructor holding my hand at all times, I felt completely safe and able to relax into the experience immediately. So, with another pool dive under my belt, it was time to take the plunge in the North Atlantic sea.

After a long walk from the hotel, I was starting to feel rather nervous, but I was determined to give it a go. What came next though, didn't exactly help to calm me down. After lifting me out of my wheelchair and onto an uncomfortable bench, Jon and two of the instructors had to try and get me into a tight, figure hugging wetsuit, which almost proved an impossible task. As I am unable to move my limbs that well, getting the tight material over my joints was a big struggle, and at one point we were all considering giving up and cancelling the dive altogether. With a bit of patience and perseverance though, we battled on and managed to get me into the suit, much to my relief. There was more discomfort to come though, as the two men then had to carry me quite some distance from the building and down to the waters edge. Looking up at the sky as I was carried between them, I wondered why on earth I'd got myself into this situation, but when we finally reached the shore and they could put me down on the water, I felt a bit better about the whole thing, and hoped that the fun was finally about to begin.

Once I was in the sea, I felt the water start to go inside my wetsuit, and I was initially worried that I was going to get too cold, but after a while I got used to the temperature and no longer felt it, much to my relief. Next, we did a couple of safety tests, including testing the mask to make sure it worked – pretty vital! – and learning a few hand signals so that I could communicate with the other guys while underwater. As soon as we'd got all this down, it was time to journey to the bottom of the ocean! Well, not quite, but we did get down quite deep, and once I'd stopped worrying about dying it was a truly awe inspiring experience. Swimming amongst shoals of brightly coloured fishes and amongst crazily shaped reefs was something I didn't think I'd ever get to experience, and there were even the remains of several small boats scattered along the ocean floor, calling it a shipwreck would be too grand, but it still made me feel like a bit of an underwater pirate.

In total I was down there for about 45 minutes before it was time to head for the surface and get lifted back up the beach. With Jon's help, I managed to get out of the wetsuit much easier than I'd got in, although it was still a bit of a struggle. So now I was back on dry land, it was time to do what all good pirates should, and head for the bar. I opted against rum though and got myself a nice cool beer and sat back to reflect on my brush with nature. Once again, if swimming and diving are your thing, I wouldn't hesitate to recommend SCUBA diving. As long as you choose a reputable company and pay attention to all the safety talks, there's no reason it can't be a very safe sport to take part in and being under water with all that stunning wildlife really is an eye opening experience.

Is it a cloud? Is it zeppelin? It's Martyn Sibley!

Hot air ballooning in Catalonia

After my journey to the bottom of the ocean, for my next hair raising adventure I took to the skies again, but this time in a much more old-fashioned contraption, a hot air balloon!

In June 2012, I was on a press trip with the Catalan Tourist Board, helping to promote accessible travel in Catalonia, as well as seeing some of the region and attempting to learn a bit of the language. In order to give us a slice of Catalan culture and help us to experience everything that the region had to offer, many different events were laid on for us during our stay, and when it was announced that going up in a hot air balloon was one of them, obviously I had my doubts. I was more cautious about going up in the balloon than I had been about flying the microlight, for the simple reason that I trust new tech much more than I trust old, and I also believed you could have more control over a plane than you could over a hot air balloon. I was also unsure whether they'd be able to secure me safely in the basket of the balloon, and unsure how I'd be able to get in it in the first place.

Aware of my doubts, the event organisers sought to dispell them. They assured me that hot air ballooning is actually a very safe method of flight and is very controlled and that while they couldn't use a hoist to get me into the basket, I could be lifted into it if I was comfortable with that. Obviously, in a perfect world I'd always have a hoist to lift me, but this is far from a perfect world, and although the people I was working with were trained in disability issues, sometimes there is only so much they can do. After my SCUBA diving experience though, I was more than used to being lifted, so I put myself - quite literally - into the hands of a man named Diego, who lifted me from my chair and into the basket.

After getting up ridiculously early that morning in order to make the most of the weather conditions, I arrived feeling rather nervous, as I hadn't had as much time to plan and research the details as I usually like to when I'm going to take part in a potentially risky activity. Once Diego lifted me into the basket though, I was sat in Recaro car seat, which had a lot of straps and harnesses to keep me in place, as well as good head and back support. Once I was safely belted up, I felt a lot safer and a bit more relaxed.

With everyone now safely contained within the basket, we left the ground and began to float gently upwards. Seeing Catalonia laid out below us was a wonderful experience, and just like my SCUBA diving adventure, there was no noise, and everything felt very calm, slow and tranquil. It was also nice to have a bit of room to think and to look at the world from a perspective you don't get to experience very often. Once we were at our planned altitude we cracked open the Prosecco and the biscuits, and it felt very decadent to be drinking at 7am, while much of the region still slept below us.

In total we were up in the air for 45 minutes before it was time to attempt what I was worried would be the hardest bit of the trip, the landing. As the wind was starting to pick up, we were forced to change course and as we landed with quite a bump, the whole basket started to tip over. The member of the support team who was at the prearranged landing spot had to run bloody fast in order to catch up with us and pull the basket back upright before it tipped over completely. As I was strapped in, I wouldn't have been able to move at all or help myself if the basket had gone over, so this was a pretty hair-raising experience, and I was very glad the guy got there just in time to save us! Despite the bumpy landing though, overall it was a fantastic journey and being able to see the countryside rolled out beneath us is something I'll never forget. In fact, I loved it so much, that I took another balloon ride in Catalonia in 2013, and thankfully this time, the landing was much smoother, and even more thankfully, there was more prosecco!

Is it a squirrel? Is it a monkey? It's Martyn Sibley!

Tree Climbing in the New Forest

In the summer of 2014 I began working with GeoCast TV again, filming an epic project to promote England's wilder spaces to disabled travellers, who might not otherwise think that these forests, mountains and moors were accessible. We filmed at six different locations across England, including Exmoor, Northumberland and the New Forest, the latter being where I got up to some monkey business. The New Forest National Park has loads of adapted facilities for disabled people and although I knew I would be trying out of a lot of them, I didn't know until a few days before that the tree climbing would involve me being up in the trees yet still in my wheelchair. I can't say that this information filled me with confidence, especially since my wheelchair weighs a massive 130kg.

When we arrived at the site and I looked up at the trees and at the thin ropes that were going to be supporting me, I got even more nervous, and needless to say I had a lot of questions! It took me a long time to trust the staff, the equipment and the general setup, but I finally let them convince me that I would be safe, they were the ones experienced in this sort of thing after all, so I decided to try and put my doubts to one side and put on a brave face for the cameras.

Once I was all rigged up, they slowly hoisted me up into the canopy and I ended up around 30 feet in the air, which definitely felt high enough considering I still thought the ropes were going to snap at any second. I definitely didn't feel weightless like I did when I had been SCUBA diving or hot air ballooning that's for sure, and I was very conscious of the sheer weight of the lump of metal that I was sitting on. After I'd been up there a few minutes though, it definitely became more enjoyable as I began to trust the equipment and accept that I wasn't going to plummet to my doom. While it was cool to be up in a tree, and obviously it wasn't something that I'd experienced before, it wasn't as fun as my other adventurous activities as there wasn't really much for me to do other than 'hang out'. Due to the craziness of a wheelchair hanging in the trees though, the photo got a lot of likes on social media, so it was great for the project, and while it isn't really something I'd volunteer to do again, I was certainly glad I'd tried it, and also very happy to be proved wrong regarding the safety of such an endeavor!

Is it a mountain goat? Is it Spiderman? It's Martyn Sibley!

Abseiling in Exmoor

In June 2012, Srin and me were invited to visit Exmoor National Park by the Calvert Trust, so that we could try out the range of accessible indoor and outdoor activities on offer. It was great that the both of us were doing something together again, and it was really good to visit a site that had so much to offer disabled people, from woodwork, to archery and horse riding. We were here to try out some more adventurous activities though, including abseiling, getting in a motorboat, and swinging through the air down the length of a huge sports hall.

After a quick explanation of what the day would entail, the pair of us transferred from our electric wheelchairs into manual ones – they have a range of manual chairs available depending on your needs – and then we were off to the abseiling site for a demonstration, after which we'd be going down ourselves! After being attached to a variety of ropes and pulleys, we were dropped over the edge of the wall backwards, while still in our manual chairs. We were then slowly lowered down the 30-foot wall vertically, to the cheers and jokes of everyone else involved. While it was definitely a thrilling experience, having done it aged 14 at the same place while on a school trip, I didn't at any point feel like I was in danger, and so I was just able to have a fun and entertaining time, coming up with appropriate song titles to fit the moment, and eventually coming up with Lady Gaga – Edge of Glory, comedy genius me!

For another activity, we relocated to a sports hall and were hoisted up into the air in slings, before being released from the guide ropes and flung through the air down the length of the sports hall. This was a pretty violent swing and it certainly made me jump and took the wind out of my sails, but definitely in a good way, I'd certainly recommend it if you want to blow away the cobwebs, though it might not be so wise to do it after a big night out!

Overall, our experience at the Calvert Trust was great fun, especially as we were together and having some laughs. I'd certainly recommend it for groups of disabled people, and many disabled groups already go there for days out or as work bonding activities. Give it a go and see it you can come up with some better song choices than me!

Is it a polar bear? Is it a husky? It's Martyn Sibley!

Skiing at La Molina

I've been waiting for the opportunity to try out skiing for a couple of years now. While I've conquered the sky and the sea, snow is something I've always been much more wary of. As I've said in previous chapters, snow for me means winter, coldness and potential chest infections lurking around every corner. Staying warm is definitely high on my list of priorities, but despite this, there are some things in life that are worth getting a bit nippy for. As with all of my more adventurous activities, I only put myself into the hands of seasoned professionals. Professionals who are going to place the highest emphasis on my safety and welfare, and are also going to provide me with the best equipment to get the job done, which in this case was warm and waterproof clothing.

My skiing dream was finally realised in December 2015 during a business trip to Barcelona. Once again, I was back in my favourite

European city in order to attend a conference on accessible tourism, set up by my long-term collaborators, the Catalan Tourist Board. The conference rather purposefully coincided with the United Nations International Day of Persons with Disabilities, which takes place every 3rd December – add it to your diaries now! Kasia and me were happily chatting away to various people at the conference, when we were introduced to a few guys from 'Barcelona Special Traveller' and an accessible skiing company called 'Train and Play', who, luckily for me, had heard on the grapevine that I was keen to try out adapted skiing. After a quick chat, we arranged for me to head off to La Molina, one of Spain's oldest ski resorts, the following day.

When we arrived the staff were nothing short of excellent. Everyone was friendly and helpful, and transferring me onto an adapted ski vehicle (basically a one-person sleigh), went as smoothly as could be expected. How exactly I was going to get up the mountain, I wasn't so sure. I didn't think it would be possible for me to use the ski lift like everyone else, but much to my surprise, I was able to sit upright while in the adapted seat and catch a ride on the ski lift. The views across the Pyrenees were stunning and I was very happy to be slowly drifting upwards into the snowy peaks, especially as I knew the journey down was going to be very different indeed!

My skiing instructor for the day was a guy called Andy, who was that great mix of consummate professional with a few drops of crazy thrown in for good measure. Andy was using his own skis, but he then held on to the back of my ski sleigh in order to guide me down the mountain.

What can I say about the ride down? It was exhilarating, thrilling, fast, and furious, in fact a lot faster than I thought it would be. Andy even did a jump with the sleigh, but one was definitely enough for me, and although I wasn't piste off (sorry!) I asked him not to do it again, as the lack of suspension meant it had given me quite a jolt. We stopped to admire the view a few times, and also did a bit of slalom skiing, which made me feel like I was taking part in the Olympics.

All in all, it was a fantastic experience and definitely one that I would recommend to other disabled people who fancy a bit of winter sport. Thankfully, due to all the warm, waterproof gear I had on, and the sheer exhilaration of the activity, I didn't get chilled to the bone either.

Is it Santa? Is it Lassie? No, it's Martyn Sibley!

Husky Dog Sleighing in Finland

After my skiing experience in Catalonia at the end of 2015, things took an even colder turn in the New Year, and I experienced temperatures I never thought I'd be able to survive. I'd been invited to Finland in order to take part in the Nordic Bloggers Experience on behalf of Disability Horizons. The convention aimed to bring together travel bloggers from all over the world in order to share stories, network and take part in seminars. As well as the seminars, the NBE also offers participants the chance to take part in some traditional Nordic experiences, which is why on the 18th January 2016, I found myself on a sleigh, attached to some Husky dogs, in -30° degree temperatures!

This experience was beyond surreal for me. I never thought I'd be able to set foot outside in such temperatures, but wrapped in what felt like a million layers as well as blankets, I was soon driving my wheelchair through the beautiful snowy landscape with another disabled travel blogger called Sanna Kalmari. Having Sanna and my fiance Kasia with me, made me feel reassured that I was actually going to survive the experience, and the beautiful snowy conditions soon took my mind off the cold. I'd never experienced weather like this before, and while it was intense, it was also very magical.

After a brief drive around in my chair, it was time to get on the sleigh. In order to get into it and stay secure, Kasia got in before me and then the driver lifted me and put me down in front of her, before quickly bundling a lot of blankets on top of us. Kasia then held onto me very tightly while the driver picked up the reins and geed up the dogs. There were six of them in total, and with a lot of barking and excitement that got off to a flying start, and we were pulled at quite a pace for around 1km, which took somewhere between 5 and 10 minutes. We were lucky to be able to go anywhere at all, as despite the ridiculously cold temperatures, there wasn't actually that much snow on the ground and at one point we didn't think we'd be able to do it at all. As luck would have it though, our driver was determined to give us our experience, and what an experience it was.

Being towed by these majestic animals was a wonderful experience for both of us, and though there were a few little bumps along the way, over all it was quite calm, especially when compared to the skiing experience I'd had just a month before. We were also lucky enough to see some reindeers, which I didn't want to get too close to those antlers! It all left me with a very Christmassy feeling, which made the experience even more surreal as Christmas had so recently been and gone.

Once we'd come to a halt, I was lifted back into my chair, and quickly made my way over to the outdoor fire to warm up, before retreating back into the house and then bus as soon as possible. While it had been a relatively short experience, I don't think I could've survived out there for much longer, and I spent the rest of the evening bundled up, to make sure I warmed up properly and didn't get ill. Despite the extreme nature of this experience though, I wouldn't hesitate to recommend sleighing, even if, like me, you're very wary of cold temperatures. It really was a fairy-tale experience, but perhaps not one that I want to repeat for a very long time, brrrr!

What Disability?

John O'Groats to Lands End Trip

In the summer of 2012 I was travelling through Europe with Filipe (one of my awesome care PA's) and Kasia – there will be a lot more on this in the next chapter – when we stopped off in Poland to meet some local disability advocates and catch up with Kasia's family. In order to gain a greater understanding of what being disabled in Poland is like, we met up with Teresa and Boguslaw, who were part of a local user-led organisation in the town of Gorzow. We interviewed the two of them in order to find out a bit more about life as a disabled person in Poland, and discovered that there was a lack of government funding, not many public transport options and that societies general attitude towards disabled people left a lot to be desired. In order to try and counteract this and raise awareness Teresa had a plan. She was going to travel around Poland in her wheelchair, covering 2500km in total, over 42 days. She would ride her wheelchair on the roads, with a support team behind her in a car and fundraise and do media appearances along the way, in order to raise awareness of what disabled people can achieve. She also planned to raise money over the course of her trip and had a number of sponsors in place, including Kasia's dad, Tadeusz, who is the Polish representative for the Canadian health supplement Toda.

Hearing about Teresa's plans was very inspiring and she quite frankly seemed pretty badass for coming up with such a brave and ambitious plan. At this point though, a plan was all it was, so when I heard from Tadeusz the following summer that Teresa was about to set off on her trip, I was quite surprised that she'd managed to put her plans into action so quickly. In order to get some much-needed media attention, Kasia and me were invited to be special guests for the last few days of the trip. As I had appeared on BBC Breakfast by this point, I had a bit more media weight behind me and I set up a crowdfunding campaign to try and raise money for Teresa from my family, friends and social media followers. In the end, we joined Teresa for the last three days of her 42-day journey, and with the sun shining down on us and lots of people waving and beeping, it turned out to be a really positive experience.

During our jaunt, we stopped off at the Woodstock Festival, obviously not the American one, but the Polish equivalent, and with around half a million people in attendance. As part of Teresa's media campaign, we all got up on stage to promote what she was doing. As they were all chatting away in Polish I had no proper idea of what was being said, but could sense the talk was quite serious and a little bit depressing, so after they had finished quite a long discussion I asked for the microphone in order to fulfill a lifetime ambition and shouted 'Woodstock, we f***ing love you!' at the crowd! Everyone went mental, screaming and cheering and I felt like a rock n roll star. While what Teresa was discussing was clearly important, when the audience is a music festival full of drunk and drugged people, serious things aren't going to go down as well, people don't only want to be preached to when they're having a good time – something Kanye West could do well to learn!

We finished off the journey with Teresa by arriving at her home town on the 4th August, and the whole experience left Kasia and me feeling hugely inspired, which of course set us both thinking…what if we did this in the UK?

Well, you can imagine what happened next. Being the mad, spur of the moment people that we are, we decided we needed only a months planning to get the project off the ground and aimed to start our journey from John O'Groats to Lands End at the beginning of September. We'd chosen to travel from the most northerly point of mainland Britain to the most Southerly as the Scottish weather was likely to be much more temperamental, so kicking off there first was likely to guarantee us better weather than arriving up there in October, while conversely October weather in Cornwall had the chance of still being relatively mild.

So, what were our reasons for setting out on such a madcap, 1,100 miles trip down the length of Britain? As you've probably realised, I always want to shine a spotlight on disabled people and get more media attention for the disability world as whole. Whether this is to raise money for charity or help the public to see disabled people in a positive light, I always try and back or get involved in projects that show disability in a new and positive light and challenge public perceptions of what disabled people can achieve. While there is plenty to get angry about with regard to the many negative ways that disabled people are still treated in the 21st century, there is also a lot to be positive about, and I believe that the public are more likely to respond positively if they are presented with positive examples, common sense really. By being positive about things it is then easier to educate people about the barriers that disabled people face on a day-today basis, such as the lack of access to many public buildings and public transport, as well as leisure activities.

On a personal level, I also wanted to challenge myself both physically and mentally, to push my boundaries while also understanding my own limits and balancing personal growth with my health. It was also a great opportunity to see more of Britain with Kasia. At this point we'd only been together for a year, but from the very offset of our friendship and then relationship we'd always clicked and been comfortable in one another's company, so she had no hesitation in jumping on her bike to join me for this crazy trip.

With so little time before our intended start date, the planning was fast paced and quite frankly mental. We had my car and a hoist, but in order to stay safe on the roads, we needed another team member to drive the car and keep an eye on us as we rode the roads. They'd also need to help out with some of my care as Kasia would quite rightly be knackered after cycling all day long. Then, we also needed to work out how we were going to gather funds for the petrol and for the accommodation we would be staying in for 30 nights. As you can see, there was a lot to organise!

In the end, we managed to recruit the legend that is Martin Gascoigne, who'd been one of my carers during my first year at uni. I knew he was a keen cyclist so he'd be able to help Kasia out with her bike and choosing appropriate cycle routes. Martin had previously helped out two guys in their attempt to cycle (pedal boats included) round the world, so he had previous experience of crazy schemes. During that trip one guy had ended up dropping out and another, named Jason Lewis had been hit by a car and hospitalized as a result, not that we let that fact put us off. In fact, I ended up Skyping Jason for some advice on mental preparation, as well as logistics and planning help.

When it came to funding, we were lucky enough to get some from the Big Lottery Fund, which at such short notice seemed like a proper coup. The project was called 'Britain's Personal Best' and was run by Steve Moore and the Big Society Network. Although later down the line the network received a lot of negative publicity, we had a good experience with them and ultimately I believe our project was one of the most socially useful projects that year.

(Not so) Little Britain

With funding and a strong team in place then, it was almost time to set off for Scotland. Kasia and me both turned 30 on the 2nd and 3rd of September respectively, which was a great beginning to the month, and we set off for Edinburgh on the 4th, staying at a hotel there over night before driving up to John O'Groats through the Highlands the next morning. Although it might sound a bit ignorant and obvious to say so, the Scottish Highlands were a LOT bigger than we had anticipated. It took us two full days of driving to reach John O'Groats, but driving through such beautiful scenery wasn't too much of a hardship, though realizing we'd be travelling through all of it again but this time outside made the enormity of what we were taking on sink in a bit more, though I wouldn't say we were nervous. I generally don't tend to get nervous about these sort of trips in advance, I always play out many scenarios in my head beforehand and make sure to prepare for the worst. Over the years, mainly due to trial and error, I've also become very in tune with my intuition and if I have a funny feeling about something I'll make sure to listen to it and change my plans accordingly.

Once we reached John O'Groats, we stayed in a hotel overnight, in order to be fully rested we could hit the road first thing the following day. The morning brought with it some typical Scottish weather, so I covered my wheelchair in my very cool and sexy rain mac, which is basically designed to cover both me and the chair, meaning my face is the only thing that's visible. At times like these I have to choose practicality over pride though, and staying dry is essential if I want to stay healthy. Kasia also donned a high vis jacket and we were ready to roll.

After the first day I think we all came to the realisation that we hadn't been prepared for how tiring this trip was going to be. My body simply wasn't used to driving that many hours straight, and the bumpy roads and uneven surfaces in the Highlands meant that by the time we finished for the day, I was feeling very achy and also pretty rough. Kasia was also exhausted, but unlike me, after a nights rest she was able to bounce back completely.

Thankfully, just in time to raise our spirits, the sun came out for the second and third days and we were able to appreciate the stunning scenery and the panoramic views across the Highlands. Many of the drivers that we passed were also very supportive at this point, smiling and waving at us, which gave us a real buzz. We also bumped (not literally) into two very well to do Englishmen who were out for a fish. In order to promote the project, which we'd named 'What Disability?' and encourage people to donate to our chosen charities, Scope, Women's Aid and Variety, I had a flag on the back of my chair and the two men stopped to talk to us about it. After explaining the project to them, they asked how they could donate, and low and behold, when I checked our donation page later that day, they'd donated a few hundred pounds! We also chatted to the people in the hotels, bed and breakfasts and restaurants that we stopped off in along the way, and right from the beginning we found everyone to be extremely friendly, welcoming and curious about what we were up to.

Despite these positive vibes though, it became evident quite early on, that this trip was starting to exhaust me to the point of danger. My muscles and bones were aching so much at the end of each day, and even the chair was struggling to do the number of miles per day that were required of it. On top of this, we also had a number of close shaves with vehicles on the road, many of which had tried to overtake Martin in the car behind us and thus nearly run into Kasia and me. Although it wasn't an easy decision to make, due to the close shaves we kept having, especially when we passed through larger towns where the motorists had less patience, we decided that from England onwards we would have to find quieter roads and only do the mileage that was possible. We'd also had a call from the Scottish police who had been very concerned about us using the A9, which made us realise all the more that our safety had to come first.

Realising that we would have to tweak our route as an when necessary, wasn't easy for me as I was so set on doing every mile, especially as we'd been raising money on the back of doing the full 1,100, but sometimes you have to do the sensible thing and it certainly reduced all of our stress levels.

For the rest of our Scottish adventure then, things were a little more laid back, although we were sometimes still on the road for 8 hours a day if we could manage it. We visited Loch Ness, though sadly couldn't find that elusive monster, and soaked up some rays in some truly gorgeous scenery. We also got to venture across the epic Forth Road Bridge and stopped off to chat to a guy who runs a café there, who told us about the popularity of the John O'Groats to Lands End trip, and told us that in the spring and summer months he meets 3 or 4 people a week who are doing it, though I was the first person he'd come across who was doing it in a wheelchair – though I hope not the last!

Green and Pleasant Lands

When we finally rolled into England, we felt a great sense of achievement. We were travelling down the western side of the country, which meant the Lake District and the Peak District, with

Manchester in between. Both National Parks were absolutely stunning to travel through, and being off of the main roads made the whole experience much calmer. Although the weather was generally a bit grey, with such stunning views it really didn't matter. We reached the highest point of our trip, quite literally, at Shap Fell in Kendal, before heading further down south to catch up with my old friend Rich from my Cov days.

When we reached the Peak District, we met up with an old friend of Martin's, Aidan, and his partner Jill, who showed us around the National Park and guided us down an old railway track that had been turned into a very smooth path, ideal for cyclists and wheelchair users. It was great to learn some of the local history and to catch up with old friends, and these calm moments in nature were some of the most memorable of the entire trip.

From the Peak District, we journeyed down through Birmingham to Worcester for our next big meet up. This time it was a family affair, as we met up with my Mum and my Stepdad Dave. We stayed in an amazing six bedroom farmhouse, complete with dog and roaring fireplace. To make the most of all this luxury we had an extra, much-needed rest day in Worcester and it was great to just kick back and relax, albeit briefly.

I'd been experiencing some problems with my chair while I was in Worcester with the family, but on the way to Bristol the motors blew completely, which given how far we'd travelled, wasn't exactly shocking, though it was certainly inconvenient. Luckily for us, I knew that the company who created by chair, Invacare, were just over the water from us in Bridgend in Wales. Although I knew they didn't service chairs, I'd been unable to locate new motors at any of the mobility shops in Bristol, so getting in touch with Invacare was the only option.

In order to get their help though, I had to kick up a bit of a fuss and tell a few white lies. Unfortunately, when we'd first approached the company about sponsoring our road trip, they hadn't been very receptive or supportive, so in order to get them to help with the repairs, I called up and simply told them that I was on holiday in Bristol and in desperate need of new motors as they'd conked out. After getting through to them, they still weren't exactly thrilled at the idea, but said they'd help if I could get to their headquarters. So that night I tweeted, via the Disability Horizons account "Off to Invacare headquarters tomorrow, let's hope they help me now". The next morning, when we rocked up in Wales the entire marketing team was there to meet us, and informed us that they'd been contacted by their American bosses and they weren't very happy with the stunt we'd pulled! This is often a problem with wheelchair companies in my opinion, many of the big ones have such a strangle hold on the market that they simply don't need to provide good customer service, as people have no choice but to use their products anyway. By challenging their good name though, I'd made a big impact and not only did they change the motors and my tyres, they did it all for free and were very keen for me to post a photo of the finished job on social media.

In the end then, it turned out to be a good bit of PR for them, as they got to be the rescue squad, and credit where credit is due, our relationship has been a very productive one since then, and we've had good dialogue ever since. This also taught me an important lesson, that sometimes you do have to cause a fuss in order to get treated the way that a loyal customer deserves, so I think all involved learnt something from the experience.

After that, we drove back to Bristol in the car and set off by wheelchair and bike towards Devon, Cornwall and the final leg of our epic trip. Devon and Cornwall were similar to the Highlands in many respects, as the roads were small, windy and there was potential danger around every corner. Things also got a bit hillier than they had been, and now it was Kasia's turn to struggle as my new motors helped me to zoom ahead without even realising it. Martin was also struggling and in many ways actually had the worst of it. Not only did he have to worry about anyone coming too fast from behind and ploughing into him, he could also see the cars coming towards us at ridiculous speeds. By Worcester he was pretty rattled already, so we were very keen to keep on going as fast as possible at this point so we could all make the finish line in one piece, mentally and physically.

In order to make things a bit easier for ourselves, we'd been staying in the same accommodation for four or five nights in a row, and then tracking back on ourselves at the end of each days driving. This way, we didn't have to go through the hassle of unloading the car every night, which saved us a good few hours.

Trekking through Devon and Cornwall did have some positives though. In order to off-road a bit but also make up for some of the mileage we missed as a result, Kasia and me hit the Camel Trail in Padstow, though being the immature children that we are, we nicknamed it the Camel Toe. About twenty minutes into our journey the lights on my wheelchair controls started flashing red, a warning that I was about to run out of battery. With no chance of car access, if I ran out of juice we were going to be well and truly screwed, as there is no way to push my chair manually as it is so heavy. As soon as we saw the flashing lights though, we turned back immediately and twenty minutes later we made it back to Martin and the car with a little bit of energy to spare, phew!

We stayed in Padstow for a few nights too, close to Rick Stein's restaurant, which meant we had plenty of lovely fish suppers. In another brush with celebrity, while we'd been in Bristol trying to sort out the issues with the chair, we'd got chatting to a group of people by the river, who turned out to be roadies for the Manic Street Preachers and were kind enough to get us free tickets for the following night. Having grown up hearing them on the radio, this was a great experience and a nice treat after so much time on the road. We also did quite a lot of media appearances on our travels too, including a fair few local radio interviews, as well as being in the Daily Mirror newspaper, and various other local papers. In the end, we managed to raise just over a £1,000 for our chosen charities, and while this wasn't as much as we hoped, we hadn't had much time to fundraise during the trip so it was to be expected.

What proved to be more valuable than the money though was the feedback that we got from disabled people. So many people were enthusiastic about the trip and told us how inspiring we were, and I still get people contacting me today who are interested in doing the same route and want my advice. I am very cautious about encouraging other people to do it though, due to the number of dangerous situations that we found ourselves in. Arguably, we rushed into the trip far sooner than we should have, and in some ways it was stupid of us to do it at all. We were certainly all very grateful by the end of it that we'd survived and not been the victims of any serious road rage incidents.

After we pulled out of Padstow, we felt like we were on the homestretch and we rolled into Lands End exactly four weeks after we'd set off. Sadly it was rainy and windy at both the start and finish of our trip, but by this point we were all so tired and strung out that we hardly noticed. We were kindly greeted by a group of ambassadors for Britain's Personal Best though, who had come along with a very welcome bottle of bubbly, along with some service users from Scope in Cornwall. Due to our exhaustion, the enormity of what we'd achieved didn't sink in until a few weeks later, and looking back it really is amazing to me that we managed to travel that far, do all those miles and actually complete the journey.

Although we'd had generally positive feedback from other disabled people, some of those who contacted us on social media hadn't been quite as supportive. A handful of people seemed quite resentful of what we were doing, and felt that as they were suffering much worse problems than a flat tyre, that we were trying to pretend being disabled in Britain was a piece of cake. While I had some sympathy with this attitude and could see where people were coming from, it also made me think a lot about the social model of disability in the coming weeks. I came to the conclusion that disabled people are just as responsible for the way they are viewed by society as everyone else is, and though we do face many barriers and a lot of prejudice, we are still partly responsible for how we are viewed by others. This is why I try to present a positive view of disability, and while I am aware that not everyone can do this due to his or her own personal circumstances, most of the time I can, and I will continue to do so for as long as possible.

To this end then, although in retrospect we were more than a little naïve about how hard the trip would be, I don't regret doing it at all.

Chapter Five – Europe

As the previous chapters attest, I get around a bit, but nowhere more so than Europe. It would sound a bit pretentious to say 'Europe is my playground' like those guys in Suede sung, but over the years parts of it have definitely become familiar territory, especially Spain. If I talked about each and every European trip I've ever been on, this chapter would quickly become long and tedious, so instead I've picked three trips that have been particularly important to me. These three life-changing trips have taken me from the boot of Italy, to the borders of Russia, and practically everywhere in between, and have stretched my boundaries more than any other continent thus far...

Aviles, the EVS, and accessible living

I first heard of the European Voluntary Service (EVS) when I was working at Scope, but with a full-time job on the go, I didn't have time to consider it properly until I'd finished working there. Initially, I thought I might be able to volunteer for a week or two, but with self employed freedom in my hands at last, I had the opportunity to do some proper research and I soon discovered it might be possible for me to live in Europe for much longer.

The process of applying for the EVS scheme turned out to be quite complex. Firstly, I needed to be selected for a project with a 'host organisation', which could be anywhere in the EU, and then I needed to work with a 'sending organisation' who would hopefully provide me with the funds for my flights, accommodation and food. While the type of project was obviously important to me, I was aware that my choice would be severely limited by accessibility. The first hurdle therefore was to find out which host organisations ran accessible projects.

To get the ball rolling, I fired off a few emails, but either I didn't hear back at all, or I heard that my needs couldn't be catered for. So after running round in circles for a few weeks, I reached out to Chris Fisher at Leonard Cheshire, a charity that helps disabled people to find volunteering opportunities. Chris then very kindly came to visit me in my London flat, and we talked through the possibilities of me volunteering with the EVS. While I would've been happy to volunteer in any number of EU countries, I really had my heart set on Spain. Sunshine, great food and amazing culture, what more could I possibly want? Chris was exceptionally helpful, we discussed my needs and developed an action plan together, and then he went off and contacted all of the Spanish agencies on my behalf, what a guy!

As the weeks passed by though, all I seemed to be receiving were negative responses. Although I don't remember a moment where I consciously gave up, it was all starting to seem like a pipe dream. None of the agencies that we had contacted had the necessary resources to host me, and that's if they even grasped my needs in the first place. All in all, things certainly weren't looking good. Then in

September 2011, when I'd pretty much given up hope, I finally received a bit of good news. The woman I heard from was called Vane (pronounced Bannae for you British folk) and she ran a project called Europa aqui (Europe Here). She told me that the organisation had recently moved to new and accessible premises and that they were based in Aviles, Spain, which was one of the northernmost parts of the country. Though she was very keen to have me on board, she recommended that instead of signing up for the maximum 12 months straight away, I should instead apply for a 2-month trial, which I could then add to later on if I wanted.

There were still some other obstacles to overcome before I could get there though. While Leonard Cheshire were keen for me to take part in the EVS scheme, they weren't an official 'sending organisation', so they couldn't sponsor me. Thankfully for me though, we were able to locate one in Leeds called 'Everything Is Possible' – good name eh – who were willing and able to support me. With all these agencies now behind me, finding funding for my needs wasn't as much of a struggle as I feared it would be. As I was only going for two months, my social care package was able to cover my care needs, my PA's flights were put into the funding budget and Vane was able to get free equipment for me from the Spanish Red Cross. It turned out that her brother was disabled, and he had volunteered with EVS in Germany, which made me feel more confident about my own trip and also confident that Vane truly understood my needs. With all the funding and logistics now in place, it was time to send the application off and cross our fingers. Finally, in January 2012, one full year after I started the process, my trip was approved and I was well and truly elated!

After getting everything signed off by the European Commission, Vane and me decided it might be wise to arrange a familiarization trip first. The point of this trip would be to go and visit the place and meet the people I'd be working with. That way, if I decided it wasn't for me, it would be a lot easier to back out, than if I'd brought all my stuff over there for a two month trip. Needless to say, I loved it. I met some of the other volunteers that I would be living with, and went along to a local carnival, which gave me a real taste of the laid-back atmosphere and the many wonderful sights and sounds of Aviles.

So with the familiarization trip a success, the date was set for me to move to Aviles on the 4th March 2012. Although I had all my costs covered for the trip, I wouldn't actually be earning any money, so I decided it would be wise to sub-let my London flat for two months. As per usual, in the run up to leaving I was well and truly focused on the logistics of the project, something that always helps to shield me from any emotional worries. Although I had never lived abroad before, good planning is an essential part of my life, and always makes me feel much calmer and less worried about things in general. Also, by this point in my life I was in my late twenties and had been living independently in London for a number of years. So although Spain would be a different kettle of fish, it wasn't quite such a big leap as it would have been a few years previously. As for the project that I would be working on, as this was quite sociable and community based, I was looking forward to it more than I was dreading it. My main task was going to be running basic English classes in a number of schools around Aviles, as well as delivering training sessions to teenagers in order to educate them about the EVS. I would also be doing some disability awareness training with local organisations, and although I didn't know it yet, I'd also have my own radio show!

When it came to my care, by this point in my life my PA's were doing two-week shift patterns, so they would be flying in and out of Aviles on a two weeks on, two weeks off basis. I obviously also took my wheelchair and charger along with me, but as the rest of my necessary equipment had been loaned to us by the Spanish Red Cross, for once I got to travel relatively lightly.

So, after a generally smooth trip, we rocked up in Aviles, unpacked and watched Aviles FC score 4 goals from my bedroom window. Not a bad start! Thankfully, my room was on the same floor as the rest of the volunteers, even though it was fully accessible and had all the equipment that I needed. On several occasions I've had to stay in a different building or hotel from those I've been working with because of accessibility issues, so it was nice to be living with all of my co-workers on this occasion. The next few days were a whirlwind of faces, places and cider. We were truly a pan-European bunch, and my Portuguese and Polish carers completed the picture nicely. As for the local cider, well that was nearly the end of me! Following local tradition, it had to be poured with the bottle by your head and the glass near your waist in order to enhance the bubbles, and then downed before the gas disappeared. Although I felt alright in the bar, when we set off home I was swerving all over the place, and with most of us in a similar state, we of course got lost, shocking behaviour eh!

The town itself was pretty accessible, and certainly no worse than the majority of similar sized towns in England. Of course there were steps into some bars and restaurants, and though it would be preferable to have none at all, as the locals were so friendly and happy to muck in and help me, it didn't prove to be too much of an issue. In terms of looks and style, it was very different from the majority of English towns. The town was just a 10-minute bus ride from the beach and 5 minutes walk from a lovely harbour. Plus it had rows and rows of brightly painted houses. With around 85,000 inhabitants it was just the right size so as not to be overwhelming, and while I did get stared at more than I would've at home, I didn't feel this to be a negative reaction, just a result of people unused to seeing electric wheelchairs.

After the dreamy nature of my first few days though, my Spanish classes began and reality hit. I realised that after studying Spanish for one year, over 14 years ago at school, was a very different kettle of fish from actually 'knowing' anything about the Spanish language. It had been a long time since I'd felt so helpless and completely out of my depth, but this reality check proved to be exactly what I needed. If I wanted to learn Spanish while I was here as I had hoped, I was going to have to work a hell of a lot harder than I currently was. My romantic notion of just 'picking up' the language by bumbling around the town and chatting to the locals was certainly crushed, but as I relish a challenge, I was ready to put in the effort and give it my best shot.

This reality check though had a knock on effect on my confidence, and after about two weeks in Aviles I hit a bit of a wall. Now that the honeymoon period was over, I remember sitting in my hostel room and feeling more than a little overwhelmed and out of my depth. Suddenly, all the things that I'd been relishing about moving to Spain seemed like massive, insurmountable barriers. I didn't speak the language, the culture was markedly different, and it dawned on me how deeply I was stuck in my English ways. Although the Spanish generally ate lunch at 2-3pm and dinner at 9-10pm, I was still trying to grab beans on toast as early and as often as I could. As I've mentioned before, food has often been one of my biggest worries when it comes to travel, and I couldn't get used to the tapas culture, so often I didn't feel full, which consequently effected my mood. As time went on though and I started to go out more and more, I got drawn into the culture and got used to the tapas, especially when I discovered Asturian Fabada, a bean dish which was markedly similar to baked beans!

As the Spanish classes continued, so did my lack of confidence. Although I was trying hard, I always felt a bit rubbish in comparison to the other international students from across the rest of Europe. In the end I decided this came back to the fact that the English are notoriously bad at languages and that we're just not given the grounding in languages that children in other European countries are. While I'm not using this as an excuse for the difficulties that I had, I do think it is an area that we as a country definitely need to work on, especially given the increasingly globalized world that we all live in. By the final weeks though, I was starting to feel more confident and my ear was starting to pick up the language in a way that I hadn't been able to before, though sadly when I went back to England, I didn't carry on learning, which no doubt set me back a bit.

Despite the slow process of my language learning, I was forging ahead with the teaching work that I'd been sent to Aviles to do. There was a definite Monday to Friday vibe to my working week, and most of the time I was either planning or delivering training workshops of various kinds. The majority of these workshops saw me going out to schools in the local area in order to run training groups with teenage kids, and discuss whether they might want to join the EVS scheme in the future, and what the different options available to them were. Basically, I was a foreigner who'd come over to sell EVS to the locals.

I also ran English classes for groups of 10-20 kids and teaching English was certainly a lot easier than learning Spanish I can tell you! I had help from the other volunteers though, so I didn't feel horribly out of my depth, and after a few weeks I'd got the knack of it.

One of the projects that I was most excited about though, was my radio show. 'Sunnier Days', as it was called, was a weekly radio show and podcast with a different theme each week, and although I was pretty sure I'd rambled incoherently in the first episode, it was a great thing to be involved in, and listening back, wasn't as bad as I'd initially feared. I did this radio show weekly from then on, as well as all of the classes that I was running or helping to run, and having Spanish classes twice a week. Despite the busyness, there was also plenty of leisure time and one of my favourite places to hang out was *Joey's,* a café run by an American guy called…you guessed it, Joey. We went there often for his delicious ham toasties, something I obviously encouraged, as I was still taking every opportunity I could to eat food that was similar to what I'd have at home. We also went on a good few trips to neighbouring towns, such as Oviedo, the capital of Asturias, which had a grander and more historic vibe, and Gijon, a coastal town with a relaxed, beachy and hippy vibe that I much preferred. It was in Oviedo though that I went to a squat party, and had my first taste of that most traditional and tasty of Spanish dishes, Paella, a big step for me considering the wide range of seafood and shellfish that it contains, I must be getting a bit braver in my old age after all!

In terms of raising awareness of disability and accessibility issues, we had a few tricks and plans up our sleeves too. We made a video about the project as a whole, and then designed and made positive stickers to give out to local businesses that had good access. We hoped that by highlighting the good ones, other businesses would be shamed into acting. I then gave a talk at the Town Hall, with the council and the media in attendance, in order to promote the project, which felt like a really positive step. Some disability activists get a bit annoyed with me at times, as they would rather focus on the bad businesses and tell them off, whereas I like to focus on the positives and encourage the good ones, hoping that in time, the bad ones will catch on. But if they don't, at the end of the day this is their loss, as they are limiting the amount of people who will visit their business.

So while the access in Aviles maybe wasn't as good as the access back in England, I have often found that access is usually better in a richer country, but the attitude of the people is often more stand offish. While the access wasn't great in Aviles, the people were very keen to help and were always warm, friendly and open. When it came to the weather though, there were many similarities between Aviles and the UK, with the climate of Aviles being similar, with lots of rain and cooler, cloudier days, but also lots of green and luscious landscapes and mountains.

Speaking of mountains, what trip would be complete without a crazy, offbeat adventure? As I've already mentioned, although some places in Aviles were accessible, not everywhere was, so any thought of getting off the beaten track and heading outside of town into the mountains seemed out of the question. If the majority of the buildings and cafes in the town weren't that accessible, what were the chances of there being accessible pathways in the mountains? I'd known before we left England that transport might be a bit of an issue, to the extent that I'd even considered bringing my car along with me on a boat, but this had proved too costly an option, and, as it was I'd been able to take the bus or the train to most places, including the neighbouring towns which was great. Getting a bus or train into the mountains though, wasn't an option, but both I and my mentor, a local Spanish guy called Ruben who worked for the Red Cross and looked like a Viking, were determined that I would get there. Ruben was a revolutionary at heart, and we'd had a lot of heated debates about politics together. In order to get the show on the road then, Ruben had a look for a van and a ramp to get me up into the mountains. A local disability organisation tried to lend us a ramp, but when testing it out I nearly tipped my chair over, which is quite a feat considering how much it weighs, so we wisely decided to go with another type from a different store. After a bit more research, Ruben hit upon the perfect location for us to visit, a collective of people who run a sustainable house high up in the mountains, with stunning views overlooking the region. The plan was that we would get a train part of the way, and then the guys from the house would come and pick us up in their van and drive us up to the house.

We arrived at the station at 1pm, and the van was there to meet us. The two women driving it were covered in tattoos and piercings and I knew straight away that it was going to be an interesting day! As I drove up the ramp to get into the van, it become clear that I wasn't going to fit, as the roof was too low. There was therefore no other option than for Filipe to lift me out of the chair and put me in the front seat, while the chair was folded and put in the boot. Having assumed that the driver, who I was now sitting next to, was Spanish, I was very surprised to hear an English accent come out of her mouth and discover she was from Southport, what a small world! To add to the hippy vibe, the van was powered by vegetable oil, which I was a bit sceptical of at first, but it managed to get us up the mountain.

Sadly, the Spanish weather was continuing its British ways, and it was bucketing it down, which restricted the views somewhat, but I could still see how beautiful and fertile the land was and taste the freshness of the air. Upon arrival, I got bumped up two steps and into the house. Although the rain prevented us from going out and exploring the stunning scenery, I had a fantastic time and it was really interesting to find out how the collective formed and learn about their activism. I shared my own disability activism with them and told them all about my blog and Disability Horizons, and while I don't think I could survive there myself – mostly due to all the healthy food they eat! – I really got what they were trying to do and was glad to be a part of it, even for a short time.

Travelling back down the mountain, I realised my Spanish adventure was about to draw to a close. I'd learnt and accomplished more during my time in Aviles than I ever thought I would, and although learning the language had been a lot harder than I thought, by the time I was ready to leave I was feeling slightly more confident about my abilities. Sadly though, when I went back to England, I didn't force myself to continue with my Spanish studies, so by the time I returned to Aviles, a year later, I had to go back over some old ground.

My second application to live and work in Aviles was on slightly different grounds. This time I wasn't applying because I was young and wanted to travel and learn about other cultures, although I still did – though perhaps I was starting to push the boundaries of 'young' – I was applying under the banner of Disability Horizons, and how my work in Aviles would help promote the magazine and disability issues in general. I was staying in the same place and working on the same project, though this time with different PA's and slightly earlier in the year, this time beginning in January.

My second stay was a bit more low key than the first, and certainly a lot less boozy. I'd realised that I'd burnt out somewhat by the end of 2012 and needed to slow down and reassess my life a bit, and Aviles thankfully gave me the time to do this. Besides all this soul-searching though, I taught English again and ran my fortnightly radio show. After these final three months, my grasp of the language became a lot stronger, and I was able to understand a lot more and string sentences together at long last.

Overall, my time in Aviles meant a lot to me. I've made lifelong friends, particularly with the project coordinator Vane, and Spain has been my favourite European country ever since. Following on from our time in Aviles the second time, Kasia and me went on to live in a tiny fishing village in Catalonia for three months, in order to get away from it all and get some work done. What we didn't realise though, was that far from being relaxing, getting away from it all was actually quite frustrating and isolating. Although it was a beautiful place, we felt cut off and unable to integrate ourselves with the locals, especially as our knowledge of the language was based on our Spanish experience, and Catalonian is quite a different kettle of fish. We did have a balcony view of the sea though, so this made up for things a little!

Since then, I've also worked regularly with the Catalan Tourist Board and visited Barcelona, my favourite European city, many times, for both work and pleasure. I really do feel very blessed to have such close ties with this amazing city, although a lot of hard work has gone into getting this far. When it comes to my knowledge of Spanish and Catalonian, I have been having lessons back home in England, but I still feel like I'm crawling along at a snails pace, though my foundation is now quite strong. So my advice here, is that if you can, learn languages at a young age, because by the time you get to my age, you've had it!

Hasta la vista, baby.

The Epic European Disability Road Trip

In between my two stays in Aviles, I wasn't just sitting at home sipping cups of tea and resting on my laurels, oh no. I was busy plotting and scheming another crazy adventure of course! In this case, The Epic European Disability Road Trip – try saying that after you've had a few – which took place in September and October 2012 and is partly the reason I felt so exhausted by the time I reached Aviles for the second time.

By this point in my career I had written so many blogs and connected with so many people via Disability Horizons and social media that I really felt I had the ear and the trust of my community. In order to harness the power of this community and once again prove what disabled people are capable of, I decided it was time to plan something I'd dreamt of doing for a couple of years, a road trip around Europe during which I'd meet and interview people and charities in order to gain a better understanding of what it is like to be a disabled person from East to West. I'd then share these interviews and findings via my blog, and try and connect my community together and get people talking, acting and learning more about disability on a global scale. I've never been one for starting small!

The original plan was to start off by heading to Lithuania – a country close to my heart as you'll soon discover- and then travel all the way down to Spain via Italy before returning to the UK, with both of my PA's, Filipe and Kasia, there to support me. I'd secured the use of a second hand, adapted campervan from a company in Coventry, which would be big enough for the three of us, as well as my equipment. After securing this, I then set up a crowdfunding campaign to help pay for our travel expenses, including food and petrol. Thankfully, I'd had a bit of experience of crowdfunding already by this point, having raised funds for my Ecourses. With this experience under my belt, I was realistic about how much we would be able to raise, and able to budget accordingly. What I wasn't able to predict though, was that on the day we launched the crowdfunding campaign, the company would have an offer for the campervan that they'd have to take. Talk about bad timing. We were then left with no choice but to change our plans. Without the campervan we'd now have to take my adapted and smaller Kia, which we couldn't fit the hoist in as well as the rest of our stuff, and as a result this meant that I would have to be lifted into bed, which Kasia wouldn't be able to do. Sadly then, Kasia had to drop out of the trip altogether, leaving just Filipe and me, which meant that it would be wise if we reduced the route drastically too.

In the end, we decided to cut the route and the length of the journey by half, but this still included visiting eight different countries in 19 days, so not too shabby at all. We even managed to slot in a visit to Kasia's hometown in Poland, to stay with her and her family, so she wouldn't be left out of the fun completely.

So with all our plans now in place, and hopefully no more bumps on the horizon, we set off for the overnight ferry from Harwich to Holland, which by a stroke of good luck and good will, we'd managed to get for free in return for a video blog about the trip on Disability Horizons. With the Kia packed up with as much stuff as we could cram into it, and an itinerary in place, we boarded the ferry with plenty of excitement and a lot of determination.

As I wasn't so confident driving in Europe at this point in my life, Filipe was responsible for doing most of the driving, which given the scale of our trip and the eight countries that we were visiting, was rather a lot! He was an absolute legend though, so apart from me doing a little bit of driving when he was tired, he was basically responsible for driving six to eight hours each day, on top of everything else that we were getting up to. Big shout out to Filipe, the man is a machine.

Once we arrived in Holland, after a rather rocky night at sea – I certainly haven't got sea legs, that's for sure, though thankfully I wasn't actually sick - we headed for Amsterdam. Our stay here was quite a laid back affair. After our bumpy night at sea we decided against sampling the whacky backy that Amsterdam is famous for, and I certainly wasn't in any hurry to head off into the Red Light

District. Perhaps 20 year old me would've been more up for getting into trouble, but as I was edging towards 30 I was more interested in rolling around the city and admiring the canals and architecture and soaking up the culture. I was also keen to get an early night, as the following morning we were set to drive 400 miles to Leipzig to go and stay with Rico, a friend from my Cov days. Thankfully, the hotel was a bargain at just £50 for the both of us and had a roll-in shower, though we did leave them with a list of possible improvements upon departure the following morning. Time and trial and error have taught me to never be afraid about speaking my mind when it comes to accessibility, and if there are obvious problems with a so called 'accessible' room – such as a large step onto the balcony – then it is wise to point them out, otherwise how will they ever learn?

The bed was comfortable though, and after a solid nights kip we felt refreshed and ready to hit the road. The drive to Leipzig certainly wasn't a short one, but with Filipe's dogged determination and some tunes on the radio, it passed smoothly enough and we were with Rico by the evening.

Though I had to be carried into his house and up to bed, we had a great time staying with Rico and he'd arranged for us to meet up with two disability organisations in Leipzig the following day. As the city had recently been through a period of redevelopment, the council had had the luxury of being able to enforce accessibility regulations, a luxury that cities with older buildings don't have. Meeting up with the two organisations, one of which was a disability youth group, I saw many similarities between the German and UK models and had some interesting conversations, especially to the affect that disabled people, if they have the opportunity, need to drive change themselves and be active in bringing about the future that they want.

After being lifted into the bath upon returning to Rico's and then lifted into bed once again, I woke up with a pressure sore and was a bit concerned about how I would cope with the rest of the days journey. This time we were heading near to Gorzow in Poland, where Kasia lived. We decided to go via Berlin and on the autobahn the pain began to get worse, so we made the decision that it was better to be safe than sorry and headed to the nearest hospital. I was seen within 20 minutes and thankfully heard that it was in its early stages and that if I put a protective pad on the area and kept an eye on it, hopefully everything would be alright. Phew! Having German doctors stare at my bum wasn't an experience I'd intended to have on this trip, but I was definitely reassured by what they said.

After my brief stint in hospital though, it was time to hit the road again and continue our journey to Poland. I'd be lying if I said all this time on the road wasn't taking its toll on us. As well as the pressure sore, I also had a bad cold and was feeling pretty exhausted in general. Our spirits were by no means broken though, and the beautiful scenery that we were constantly passing through helped to keep our spirits up.

By the time we reached Kasia's house, it was pitch black outside and our satnav had sent us down a tiny farm track in what seemed to be the middle of nowhere. As we continued cautiously down this road we saw black land rovers parked to the side and became convinced we'd driven into some sort of gangster meeting and were about to get attacked and murdered! Of course, no such thing happened and we eventually found Kasia's house, much to our relief.

The first day with Kasia's family was a much-needed break from the stresses of the trip thus far, and we spent the day enjoying their beautiful garden, visiting a nearby lake and playing music around a campfire at night. I'd dusted off my harmonica and brought it along for the ride, so I just about managed to blag my way through some of the musical numbers. It was a proper outdoor experience and it was great to have some fresh air after so many hours on the road. After our day of relaxation though, it was time to get busy again. The first thing on the list was a media conference with a disability organisation who had started a petition for accessible buses in Gorzow, which had gained a lot of media attention in Poland. I was asked to speak at the conference, which was a first for me and therefore a bit nerve-wrecking, but definitely something I gained a lot from doing.

Afterwards, I met up with Bogdan, an ex-speedway champion and Teresa, who you may remember from the Adventure chapter. This was the first time I met her and first heard about her plans to travel around Poland in her wheelchair in order to promote disability awareness. At this point, I obviously didn't know how much this project was going to impact on my own life, so it's great to look back and realise how meeting one person for a chat can have such a huge impact on your life. This is what I love about what I do, I never know where the next idea is going to come from, or what is waiting round the corner to influence and inspire me. With the interviews done, it was time to say goodbye to Kasia and her family – little did I know at this point, but this would be the first of many, many visits to stay with them. But for now it was time to hit the road again and travel on to Gdansk to stay with another old PA of mine, Gabi. This was more of a social visit, and involved a bit more eating and drinking which I never complain about. We did however get a chance to check out the town centre, though I spent a lot of time resting up and trying to recover from my lingering cold, as the next day was going to be a big one.

One of the things I had been looking forward to most about this trip, although it was bringing up mixed emotions, was visiting Vilnius,

Lithuania. My Granddad, who had sadly passed away when I was 14, was Lithuanian and had been forced to flee his country because of the Russians and the Nazis. Although he had rarely talked about it, and I had been too young at the time to dig much further, his story was a tragic one, as many stories were during this awful time. At the age of 19 he had been hiding out in a forest in order to try and escape the Nazis, but had been captured and imprisoned in a prisoner of war camp in Germany. Thankfully, he managed to survive until the Allied victory, but after the war things weren't much easier either, and he was forced by circumstances to clear up dead bodies in return for food to keep himself alive. Eventually though, in 1946 he managed to make his way to England as a refugee and settled in Cambridge, where he became head butler at Emmanuel College in Cambridge university, where a painting of him serving hangs to this day. I'd never visited the country of my Granddad's birth, and I was very eager to see what it was like and learn more about where he'd grown up. I regret not asking him more questions about his war time experiences before he died, but as with most things, we never think to ask until it is too late. Plus, he seemed keen to just focus on the present and his life in England, which, given the horrifying nature of the things he must have seen is fair enough.

After an eight-hour drive, we arrived in Vilnius quite late and struggled to find a restaurant that was accessible. After catching up with some sleep on Sunday morning though, we met up with Gitana, a PA of my friend Matthew, and she and her partner and their daughter showed us around the city. Vilnius turned out to be a lovely city, with many interesting sites to see, including the Presidents Palace and St Anne's Church. It was great to finally see the place that my Granddad would've known as a child and a teenager and get some perspective as to what his life would have been like before the Second World War. While there I also met up with the society for Disabled People and learnt a bit about what it was like to be disabled in Lithuania. The country has certainly been through a lot over the years, and while many of the restaurants and bars in Vilnius weren't very accessible, I think with time, things can only get better.

So after a few days in my ancestral homeland, it was back to Poland for a flying visit to Warsaw, where we ran into some accommodation problems, as we couldn't get the roll-in shower that we had initially been promised. Despite this though, I finally felt like I was on top of things, as the rest of our accommodation from this point on had been booked and sorted and all of our appointments were also arranged. My cold was finally starting to clear up too, though Filipe wasn't feeling too chipper and it was at this point that I had to take over the driving for a bit.

After Warsaw, it was on to Krakow, where I met up with the sister of Basia, a woman I had originally met while on a training course in Turkey straight after my EVS experience in Aviles. Basia and her sister Gosia run an organisation called MMS that works in the social field with European partners. Together, we met up with a disability arts group called 'Foundation Artes', which was a fun and educational experience and in stark contrast to what we were planning to do the following day.

Between Krakow and our next stop, Prague, we had decided to visit Auschwitz concentration camp. Visiting the site of so many atrocities was an eerie experience and trying to comprehend the sheer scale of the horrors and crimes that were perpetrated is very difficult to get your head around. As well as the mass extermination of the Jews, the Nazis also murdered many other groups of people who did not conform to their idea of a 'perfect' Aryan race, including many disabled people. A fact that really hit home when we visited the medical areas of the site, where many people were tortured and experimented on. It was a strange experience, but I'm glad I took the time to visit and it was hugely educational and increased my knowledge of a period in history that we must never forget or return to.

After Auschwitz then, it was time to head to Prague, perhaps one of the most cobbled cities in the world, and thus a bit of a headache – literally – for wheelchair users. For most of our visit my brain was rattling around in my skull, and although it was one of the most beautiful cities I have ever visited, with the cobbles often impossible to avoid, it was quite hard going. While we were here though, we met up with a disability group called POV, who work with the government to create laws, and with university students to teach them the best ways to implement these laws through architecture and town planning. They were a really proactive organisation, and accessibility in Prague as a whole (minus the cobbles) was pretty much the same as in the UK. By this point in our trip though, we were starting to feel weary and I was glad that in a few days time we would be heading home, though we were going to be staying in both Germany and Brussels on the way.

In Germany we stayed in the apartment of a friend of Kasia's, before stopping off in Brussels the next day. While in Brussels we had a moment of rebellion and tried to gatecrash the parliament, but unfortunately no one would come out to see us, so being the persistent pair that we are, we decided to crash the European Disability Forum instead. Here, we had more luck and managed to get a chat with one of the forum members and a photo to prove it and put on the blog, not a bad days work!

In Brussels then, we had reached the end of our Epic European Disability Road Trip and it was time to head back to Blighty. Overall, despite some hotel issues, a couple of bad colds, and a lot of last minute planning that had sometimes left me feeling drained, the trip had actually gone relatively smoothly and we'd managed to cram a hell of a lot into just over two weeks.

Europe Without Barriers

In June 2014, I was invited to speak in Brussels on behalf of the European Network for Accessible Tourism (ENAT) and out of this one talk, sprung my involvement with Europe Without Barriers. I was invited to join the project in early 2015, just as Kasia and me were planning a month long trip to Barcelona to work with the hotel I had been partnering with, MIC Sant Jordi. In return for some marketing work, we were going to be staying there for a month free of charge, while also working with the Catalan Tourist Board, which clearly isn't bad work if you can get it!

I realise, that much of what I am going to relay in this section of the book is going to sound endlessly glamorous and make me sound like some sort of European playboy. The truth is though, I have got these opportunities because of years of hard graft, and nothing has been given to me for free. My relationship with this particular hotel has been built up over a number of years, and I was asked to get involved in the Europe Without Barriers trip because of all of the work, often for free or little pay, that I have done in the accessible tourism field. So while much of this coming section may sound glamorous, it has been hard won, and in truth, we had to work exceptionally hard throughout the trip in order to earn our keep, so it wasn't all sun and cocktails!

Before setting up camp in Barcelona though, Kasia and me had decided to go back to Aviles, to visit our old friends from the EVS days. It was great seeing Vane again and seeing how the project was moving forward, and also good to head back to Joey's for one of his famous ham toasties. After staying for a few days though, it was time to head for sunny Barcelona and get our heads down and some work done. Though we also got a chance to explore the coast and generally mooch around a city that we know and love so much now. Happy days!

The month soon came to a close, and it was time to join the rest of the Europe Without Barriers crew and get started on the project, which we were pretty excited about. It was also great because this trip made up for the part of the Epic European Disability Road Trip that Kasia and me had been unable to do together because of the campervan falling through.

So, what was the point of the Europe Without Barriers project? Well, let me tell you! The participants, myself included, had been selected from all over Europe and from a variety of different accessible tourism professions. The idea was that we would visit five different countries, stay in four hotels, and visit multiple tourist destinations along the way. The aim then was to create accessible itineraries that other disabled travellers could use in the future, and do this by collaborating together and pooling information from our different perspectives and using our specialist areas of interest. My own particular role was to look at and test everything from a wheelchair users perspective, as well as feeding back any issues that people with other impairments may have, and to use my blogging skills to document the trip and promote it via social media. Kasia was also involved too, and was one of the official photographers for the trip. Other people's roles varied, from the very in depth and analytical measure of ramp gradients and signage, to general auditing and data. Thankfully though, I didn't have to get involved in anything on the technical side, but I certainly was kept busy throughout the project, with early mornings and late nights as standard. But I'm getting ahead of myself now; lets get back to mine and Kasia's departure from Barcelona.

From Barcelona, we drove to Cannes where we'd found a cheap hotel to stay at for one night. We managed to get out and have a look around the glamorous centre of town too and generally soak up the laid back vibe. Then the following day we drove from Cannes to Folonica, for what would be my first time in Italy. As a pizza and pasta fanatic, I was majorly excited about this. For once I was in a country where I was guaranteed to love the food!

We arrived at 'i girasoli' – the sunflower hotel – on the 5th June for day one of the project. Our first 'meeting' was over lunch in the hot Italian sunshine, with the project coordinators. Although we had already been sent the itinerary, it was good to learn a bit more about the project and exactly what it was that we were expected to do. We then headed back to our room – accessible of course – to cool off, before meeting the rest of the team over a delicious Italian dinner. The majority of the people in the group were Italian, as well as two Poles (including Kasia), one Latvian and myself, the sole English person. We were going to be spending five nights at the i girasoli, which was in Tuscany, so we settled in and got ourselves a good nights sleep in preparation for the activities that were to come.

The next four days were a whirlwind of planning, activities, and the baking hot Italian sun. All in all we visited Arezzo, Florence, Siena, Perugia and Assisi and checked out some of Italy's top tourist attractions, including the famous Duomo church in Florence, where we were lucky enough to see a wedding taking place. As this was a pilot project, there was lots of talk about the rating system that we would apply to the places that we visited and a lot of discussion of metrics. As this was the first time, our analysis was inevitably going to be a work in progress. Despite the work though, so much of this trip around Italy was a dream come true, although the weather was a little too hot at times, going to see so many historic and utterly beautiful sites was an amazing experience and I just felt so lucky to be involved in the project.

The i girasoli was a fantastic hotel, despite being seemingly in the middle of nowhere. Actually, it was very well connected to five local cities in the Tuscany region and had 50 adapted rooms for disabled tourists, which is a lot more than the average hotel. Our days usually ended with dinner in the hotel and a debrief meeting, although we had the odd little party as well. After five nights though, it was time to move on to Slovenia. It was a 7-hour drive to our second hotel in Catez and we were lucky enough to pass through Venice on the way, though sadly we didn't have time to stop off here. Our second hotel was the Terme and after getting ourselves showered and settled in, we both slept like babies.

The next day was a full on pampering session for me, something I had never experienced in my life before. I was treated to a Thai massage, a sauna and steam room and a float around the bubbly swimming pool. I really was feeling like the cat who got the cream at this point. What is important to point out though, is that this is certainly not a regular occurrence for me, most of my days are 9 to 5, slogging away at my desk, but it is luxuries and treats like this, that make all that slog worth every minute. We also passed some of the morning measuring the distance from the hotel to other key amenities and collecting data that would be useful for our eventual itinerary. On day two in Slovenia, we left the comfort of the Spa hotel and head out to Ljublijana, the capital city of Slovenia. It was a very beautiful city centre, with lots of lovely cafes and bars and stunning scenery, and in the main it was quite accessible too, which is obviously always a bonus!

Next, it was time to take a trip into the darkness of the Postojna Caves. I didn't think I would get the chance to visit caves, as they're generally naturally inaccessible places for people in wheelchairs. These caves though had a train that we thought I would be able to get on. Unfortunately, upon arriving it appeared that my wheelchair was just too large and too heavy to get on board, but I'm always willing to be manhandled if it means I can take part in a new experience, so I let some of the staff lift me out of my chair and into the train, scary as it was. Then with Kasia holding me up, we were off into the wondrous cave system. It was truly an awe-inspiring sight and wonderful to experience something new that I thought I never would. Although it was a shame that the train wasn't accessible for my chair, there are some instances where this is nigh on impossible, and the fact that they were willing to help lift me into the train was excellent. My friend from the project, an Italian media guru named Stefano Massoli, who I'd been singing Italian opera with a few days before, – no alcohol was involved, honest! – helped to film us inside the cave so we could keep up with our blogging activities.

After our underground adventures, our stay in Slovenia involved one final day trip, this time across the border into Croatia. We were headed for Zagreb, and this is where we ran into a bit of attitude from the tour guide, who was annoyed that we hadn't informed him that our group would contain wheelchair users. We managed to smooth him out though, calmly but assertively and enjoyed our tour of Zagreb's historic and cultural sites. We then took a trip in an accessible funicular, which was a pretty hot experience but offered us some stunning views and lunch at the top was very agreeable too! Before travelling back to the Spa hotel for our final night, and driving to Auronzo Di Cadore, in the Italian Dolomite Mountains the following morning.

This was an absolutely beautiful place to stay and our accommodation was a 5 storey, fully renovated house with 9 adapted apartments, which were all accessible via a central lift system. As it had been a long drive – from morning to late afternoon - when we arrived we had some chill time, before heading straight out for pizza, wine and a good time. The next day, much to some people's relief, saw the first rain of the entire trip and a welcome, slightly cooler break in the weather. We waited until it stopped to head out for a morning walk to the tourist office, but then it started up again and was relentless for the rest of the day. That's what you get for staying in the mountains I guess.

After breakfast though, we headed by bus further into the mountains and managed to outrun the rain. We stopped by the stunning lake Misurina for lunch and rolled around the edge of the water, taking in the beautiful views. We spent the rest of the day relaxing and chilling out, which was very much needed, especially as we had another 6 hour drive ahead of us in the morning.

By this point of the trip, we were all feeling pretty tired, but plodded on nonetheless and were reenergized when we saw the mountaintop location of our final destination, the hotel Viktor in Vicktorsberg, Austria. The following day we travelled out to Lake Constance to enjoy an accessible boat ride. As a kid, and even as an adult, there were certain things I thought I'd just never be able to do, but this trip kept smashing down barriers, and feeling the wind whipping through my hair while travelling across the water really made me feel like I could achieve anything if I set my mind to it.

The final day though proved that when accessibility fails, barriers spring back up and there is nothing you can do to knock them down. After checking out of the hotel, we travelled to Neuschwanstein Castle, which was apparently the inspiration for the Disney castle!

Upon arrival we discovered that they couldn't transport electric wheelchairs up the mountain and people with wheelchairs had to be separated from the rest of their group. This felt like a huge let down, especially on the final day, because by this point we were all so tired. So unfortunately, we had to say goodbye to the rest of the group earlier than expected.

Overall though, this was a small moment of negativity in what was a hugely positive trip. It did highlight that we need to keep up the good fight, but in general I'd done many things that I never thought I'd get the opportunity to do. From Austria, we then drove on to Poland to spend two weeks with Kasia's family, before heading back home to the UK. We'd left in late April and got back again in July, and my beloved Kia definitely had the scars to prove it. When we checked the tyres upon returning, we noticed how worn down they'd got and that we were actually quite lucky we hadn't been in an accident. But I guess that's what you get when you're on the road for months on end and drive up two or three mountains in the process!

In the end though, this had been the trip of a lifetime and I'd experienced so much in such a relatively short space of time. I'd learnt loads more about Europe, and confirmed that some of the European stereotypes were indeed true – Spaniards have a very different concept of time, Italians love chatting over coffee, and us English are constantly laughed at for our over the top politeness. Going around beautiful countries and making videos really was a dream come true, and it seemed like I was having the Michael Palin/Judith Chalmers moment that I'd always dreamed of. Like I've said before though, I don't expect every disabled person to do what I do, and I only do it because I love it. But if it inspires anyone at all, even to do something smaller in their life, then that is good enough for me.

Chapter Six – Japan

Up until now, most of the trips that feature in this book have been mostly for pleasure, to promote disability awareness and accessibility, or in order to achieve personal goals. In early 2014 though, I went on my first major work trip outside of Europe, and took part in what proved to be one of the most gruelling projects I've been involved with to date.

In order to explain why I was invited to Japan, things are going to have to get a bit technical and jargon heavy, but let's just get this over with so we can move on to the good stuff! I was invited to Japan, a country I had never visited before, but was desperate to see, by the National Centre for Voluntary Organisations (NCVO), who were recruiting for this project on behalf of its organiser, the Cabinet Office of Japan. NCVO were involved in setting up an international exchange between the UK, New Zealand, Denmark and Japan, whose aim was to bring together people from different Not-For-Profit Organisations (NPOs) in these countries, in order for them to share resources, ideas and best practice. This meant that groups from the UK, New Zealand and Denmark were being flown to Tokyo and the whole trip was going to be funded by the Japanese government. Although I was stoked about the idea of a fully-funded trip to Japan,

I wasn't aware before jetting off, exactly what I was letting myself in for, and the schedule turned out to be very gruelling. But let's begin at the beginning shall we?

In order to learn about the best practice of three other countries, countries that Japan considered to be among the best in the world when it came to civil society issues, about 12 people from each of the chosen countries were to be flown to Tokyo for 10 days of talks, conferences and workshops. The Japanese government had divided civil society into three separate categories for the purpose of this project: Older People, Young People and Disabled People. While this may seem a bit of a basic definition, and there are obviously massive overlaps between the three categories, it was one of the simplest ways of carving up a complex program. Basically, Japan wanted to look at any areas where they felt people were marginalised or socially excluded from wider society, and find solutions to these problems.

So, why was I called on for such an official and complex sounding conference I hear you ask? Well, to be fair, that is what I asked myself too, but perhaps I am doing myself a disservice. I had recently been on the Nexters program in London, which was set up to encourage social enterprise, and this, combined with taking part in the EVS scheme in Aviles, meant that I was on the NCVO's radar. So before I knew it, I was asked whether I'd be interested in being one of the UK's 12 delegates. After learning a bit more about the program and the process of applying, I understood that if you wanted to apply to be one of the delegates, you had to go through quite a tough application process, and that most of the people who had applied worked at national and grassroots charities.

There was one catch though, none of the UK delegates were disabled, and as one of the focus groups was going to, well, focus on disability, that was a bit of problem. At this point you may think it's fair to scream tokenism at me, and say that I was picked merely for my wheelchair as opposed to my experience, but in truth, I did need to have the experience too, and I did have it. While there was clearly an element of me being let in via the back door, as most people had already completed their applications and been selected by the time I was even contacted, I was still chosen because I had a good understanding of politics and economics and the experience to back it up. And in the end, my attitude was…tokenism, or no tokenism, I'm going to flippin' Japan!!

After saying yes to the project, I got various information packs and itineraries sent to me, but as usual before a trip, it was the logistics that were concerning me. It took quite a while to sort out the hotels, equipment and flights, which had a detrimental effect on my understanding of the project as a whole. Kasia and me were feeling pretty laid back about the whole thing before setting off and we were of the attitude 'we'll just see what happens when we get there'. It was this attitude though, that led us to do a bit of last minute panic buying at the airport. When we arrived at Heathrow, we met up with the other delegates and our group leader and thankfully we were reminded that it is traditional to exchange gifts when first meeting someone in Japanese culture, so we quickly loaded up on fancy tins of sweets to stow in our hand luggage.

The other thing we'd clearly failed to anticipate was the fact that everyone else was wearing a suit. Stupidly, I hadn't thought through the fact that there would be formal events and had failed to pack mine. The only shirt I'd brought with me was an off-white, almost greyish number that had to be paired with a navy blue jumper in order to look half decent, and I did feel a bit of a fool wearing it when everyone else was suited and booted. It is at times like this that I'm guilty of hoping that people think I'm incapable of wearing a suit because of my disability. Hey, I've got to use it to my advantage sometimes, right?

Tokyo Drift

The flight was very long and more than a little uncomfortable as I was unable to move, but we finally reached our hotel at 2pm Tokyo time, having missed a night's sleep during the flight. Our intention was to have a short nap and then go out for dinner and acclimatize, but after falling asleep there was no chance we were getting up again, and in fact we didn't wake up until 5.30am the following morning. This mega sleep did us good though, and we felt ready to tackle everything the day was going to throw at us, though we didn't realise quite how much it was going to throw.

Our first day began with a welcome reception at 9am and a chance to meet the other delegates, and we didn't stop until late that evening. There were speeches, seminars and a lot of information to soak up, which left us both exhausted by the end of the day. Our first four days in Tokyo revolved around this initial conference, in which we met up with other people from the not-for-profit sector and exchanged ideas. We were then split into a range of different groups and asked to come up with solutions to different problems that faced that sector. At the end of this four-day seminar, we were then asked to present our group findings during a large ceremony, which was more than a little nerve-wrecking, but fortunately it went by in a bit of a blur given the intensity of the week up until that point. We also went out and visited some of our target groups during this four day period, but most of our work was within the conference space, taking part in brainstorming activities and the like.

Our hotel was a typical example of Tokyo living, high up and overlooking the glittering city below. The organisers had arranged a shower chair and hoist for me, and although I wasn't able to use it, as I don't find lying in the bath particularly comfortable, there was an adapted bathtub with an extendable shower hose and drains in the centre of the room. This meant I could shower or bathe, which was an excellent feature and typical of the high standard of tech and design that you find in Japan.

On day five of our trip, after delivering our findings the evening before, we moved to a different conference centre, right next to Tokyo's Olympic Park. All of the other delegates had moved to a hotel closer to the site, but unfortunately for us, this second hotel was inaccessible, meaning Kasia and me had to stay put. As a result, we missed out on some fun nights and bonding sessions, which slowed the speed at which we became integrated into the group as a whole. It didn't hold us back forever though, and before long we were going out for late-night karaoke sessions and singing Bryan Adams, One Direction and the groups favourite karaoke tune, *Africa* by Toto. There's something about being in a foreign country with other visitors that really brings out a feeling of comradery, and wailing Bryan Adams with a group of people from all around the world was a fantastic experience. Having a common cause made it feel like we were on some sort of scout camp, and while many of the Japanese delegates didn't mingle as much as everyone else, simply because they had homes to go to, we still all got to know each other reasonably well over the course of the two weeks.

After five days of working hard, we finally got a day off to go out and explore the sights and sounds of Tokyo, and luckily for us, I knew just the right person to show us around. When I was 13 years old, an exchange student from Tokyo had come to my school in Cambridge. Haruka and me had sat next to each other for the year he was there and we'd become good friends. Though we hadn't spoken or seen each other since he'd left, I'd managed to track him down on Facebook and was really happy to hear that he was still in Tokyo and able to meet up with us. I must say, my excitement at meeting him again was mixed with apprehension in case we didn't get along, but thankfully, after some initial awkwardness, we slipped back into our old ways and got on like a house on fire. We'd both been pretty busy since that year at school, so we had a lot to chat about, and as he obviously hadn't met Kasia before, there was more than enough conversation to go round. As Tokyo was his hometown, Haruka gave us an excellent tour, taking us to see all the hotspots and it was fantastic to see this amazing, futuristic city through the eyes of someone who had lived there for most of their life.

Though a day certainly wasn't enough to appreciate all that Tokyo had to offer, it was sadly all that we had, and it was now time to move onto Hiroshima. We were due to spend six days in Hiroshima for the second part of our two week trip, and me and Kasia were going to be put up by a family with a disabled child for one of these nights.

First though, it was time to board the bullet train! Travelling at over 300km an hour was certainly an experience, but much like being on a plane, it was hard to actually get a feel of the speed that we were travelling at. Just four hours later though we were at a local government welcome reception, packed full of new faces and new ideas.

Thankfully, in Hiroshima, we had more evenings free than we'd had in Tokyo, which meant we had a chance to explore the city's horrific modern history. On the 6th August 1945, America, with the backing of the UK, dropped an atomic bomb on Hiroshima, which eventually killed an estimated 140,000 people – as a result of the initial explosion and due to injuries and radiation. The combined effect of this and another bomb that was dropped on Nagasaki, led to Japan surrendering on the 15th August, thus ending the Second World War. Though, there are still debates about whether the bombings were necessary in order to bring about Japan's surrender, and of course there is much debate about the ethics of the bombings too. As a result of the bomb, the centre of Hiroshima was completely flattened, and with no money to rebuild, the city had to wait for funding from the US forces that had occupied Japan. Eventually, the money arrived, but it still took around 3 years for the city to be rebuilt. Due to the type of bomb that was dropped on Hiroshima though, and the fact that the resultant fireball didn't touch the ground, the city did not suffer from long term radiation problems in the way that Chernobyl would, 41 years later, which meant that most of the city's survivors were able to return as soon as the infrastructure was rebuilt. In order to learn about this, and much more, we headed to the Atomic Bomb Memorial Park. At its centre, is a flame that Japan will keep burning until all of the world's nuclear weapons are destroyed, which is a lovely thought, though the pessimist in me fears that it will never go out. We also visited the A-bomb museum, and after my visit to Auschwitz a few years earlier, it was horrible and very affecting to be reminded of the horrors that humans are capable of inflicting on one another. The fact that no nuclear bombs have been dropped since though, is something to give us hope.

In order to cheer ourselves up a bit after this sad day, we went out and sampled the traditional dish of Hiroshima, which is a local version of Okonomiyaki, a Japanese savoury pancake, the ingredients of which are served in layers in Hiroshima, rather than mixed as they are generally. The ingredients included cabbage, batter, pork and noodles and I must say, that much to surprise and despite my fussy food habits, I found it delicious. In fact, during the whole trip I got along much better than I imagined I would. To be fair, I stuck mostly to chicken and rice combos, as I knew that I'd like them, but I did experiment on the first night and ordered a mixed tempura, despite not knowing what tempura was. Sadly though, it wasn't my favourite and after nibbling my way through some of it, I left the rest untouched. But hey ho, if you don't try, you'll never know. Kasia on the other hand, was having a fantastic time. She's basically the opposite of me when it comes to food, as she's a vegetarian and into healthy eating. So she absolutely loved the choice of vegetable, noodle and rice dishes on offer, and chomped her way through a much wider variety of things than I did. Thankfully though, there were a fair few different chicken curries for me to try, so I didn't starve, and I must say that as chicken curries go, these were some of the best I'd ever tasted.

Aside from the history and food though, we were actually there to do work, and work we did. It was only the disability section of the project that had been sent to Hiroshima and we were there to look at the education, employment and social aspects of living and what could be done to improve things for disabled people. In order to do this, we visited a number of different projects during our week there, including a sheltered employment workspace and social centre. Our job was to analyse what we had seen and brainstorm any potential improvements and innovations that could be made. We would be delivering our findings during a big ceremony upon our return to Tokyo, so it was vital that we put the work in now so that we had something to show for ourselves.

In order to get a genuine taste of what life is like for a disabled person in Japan, we stayed with a Japanese father and his disabled son for 24 hours. The son, Nitsuki, developed his disability as his mother had been suffering from cancer while she was pregnant with him. Sadly, she died soon after Nitsuki was born and he was left in the care of his amazing father, Nao-San, who set up a home for disabled people in his local community. After picking us up in his adapted vehicle, Nao-San drove us to the San Frecce football stadium to watch our first (and only) Japanese football match. Much to the crowds delight, the local team won 2-1 after a stunning overhead kick and the fans certainly knew how to celebrate their victory! Much to my surprise, Nao-San also bought me a football shirt, which further highlights the generosity of all of the Japanese people that I had met thus far.

Next on the itinerary was a visit to the group home that Nao-San had set up, which not only benefitted his son, but also the people of the local area. The staff and service users were incredibly kind and generous and gave Kasia a Kimono, which was a very thoughtful and lovely gift. In fact, they made us feel like some sort of celebrity couple and were thrilled to hear that we were engaged and asked many questions about life back in England. Nao-San's group home operates as a day centre as a well as a home for overnight boarders, so we got to meet a cross-section of the local community, which was great for our research as well as our broader understanding of how disability services worked in Japan. Soon though, it was time to head to the family home, where we met Nitsuki, who was there with his friend, another young disabled boy, as well as the boys' parents. The house was totally accessible and Nao-San had put on a huge spread of delicious food and Sake, which I struggled my way through, due to my pickiness and small appetite. Everyone was so welcoming, but we did have some communication issues, especially as we were trying to talk to the dad of the other boy via Google Translate, which isn't always the most accurate of tools! In all of our conferences up until this point, we'd heard Denmark and New Zealand called the same name they were in English, but the UK was given a name that we hadn't been able to understand. So we decided to ask what it was through Google Translate, but much to our amusement the voice recognition software heard this as 'what is a Japanese sandwich?'

There were lots of funny miscommunication moments like this, but as everyone was so friendly and helpful, it didn't cause us any serious problems.

An even more surreal moment came when Nao-San disappeared for a while and returned to a banging soundtrack of Euro Disco music dressed up as Mickey Mouse, all without any warning. Nitsuki was 10 years old, but the nature of his disability meant that he responded more to visuals and music than he did to conversation, so Nao-San was going wild, dancing, playing a trumpet and laughing for his son's amusement. While this was great for Nitsuki, it was a little unnerving for us, especially when Nao-San was joined by a giant helium fish, that with the aid of a remote control was flying around the house and slapping its back fin. Considering my former fears about Mickey Mouse eating me, it was a wonder I kept it together! But there was no denying that Nao-San was an amazing father, and he made us feel extremely welcome in his home and his community.

After we'd gathered all the necessary data from the social projects we'd visited, it was time to head back to Tokyo to deliver our findings to the rest of the group. It was great to meet up with everyone again, and for our final night, each country was asked to put on a bit of a show for the others. This saw the Japanese contingent performing a traditional song and dance piece, while the Denmark delegates performed a Danish version of Frere Jacque. The Kiwis gave the most impressive performance by performing the Haka, the traditional war cry of the Maori people, which is performed at the start of every rugby match by the New Zealand All Blacks. Seeing a group of people, who up until this point I'd just seen in business clothes and acting professionally, suddenly take on the passion, anger and swagger that is required for any good Haka, was quite a shock and definitely the best performance of the night. When it came to our turn though, things got a little cheesy. We'd decided to sing John Lennon's *Imagine* and while we did so, we all held a single flower, which we each gave to a member of the audience while we were singing. Cringe! As I wasn't able to get down off the stage easily, someone came up to me to collect their flower, which only seemed to make things seem more cringeworthy. We'd performed it with our tongues firmly in our cheeks though and to be fair, the Danish song wasn't exactly cheese free.

With the final presentation in the bag, it was nearly time to say goodbye to Japan. Our visit had been more intense than we'd ever imagined, with two weeks of early mornings, long days and a lot of hard graft and networking. Aside from the work though, it had also been very different culturally, and it had been great to experience so many new things and see the world from a different perspective. Culturally speaking, in my opinion people have a lot more respect for one another in Japan than they do in other European countries, which can be seen in the habit of giving gifts and bowing when meeting people. Though the bowing had caused me some trouble, as being in a wheelchair made it a bit trickier. When we received our certificates at the end of the two weeks, I discovered that if I lent back while going up the ramp to the stage, which I naturally do anyway, I could then very quickly lean as far forward as possible, and pass this off as a bow. The trials and tribulations of being disabled eh!

This respect for others is often misconstrued in the West, particularly when it comes to the East Asian custom of wearing face masks when out in public. We generally assume these masks are worn because people do not wish to catch germs, but in fact it is because they do not wish to pass theirs on to others. In comparison, I think much of Western culture is geared towards making us individually minded and often materialistic, which for better or for worse, can lead to the odd culture clash.

Perhaps detrimentally though, this tendency to look after your own and those in the wider community can lead to a bit more closeting of disabled people within the family unit. While having your parents look after you for as long as they can if you are disabled, is just how things are done over there, it can be argued that this attitude denies people their independence and may have a detrimental effect on their personal growth. As with most things though, I believe that with time this attitude will start to shift and disabled people will be more visible and more independent in Japan as a whole.

As for the effect that the trip had on me, from Japan onwards I have been offered many more working trips abroad, and while these are generally under the umbrella of going to a place, delivering services and having my expenses paid, as opposed to getting paid an actual salary, this does, at the very least give me the opportunity to travel more without the financial strain. I also feel more comfortable and confident travelling now than I ever did, and it takes less brainpower and generally much less stress for me to plan a trip. The social consequences are also a nice benefit, and since leaving Japan, Kasia and me have met up with the delegates including some Danish guys a couple of times, including going to a karaoke bar in London to sings all those Bryan Adams tunes again.

All in all, the Japan trip added another useful string to my bow and helped move my career forward in new and interesting directions. Not only did it boost my confidence, but being thrown in the deep end with regard to what was expected of me for those two weeks, has now made me feel that I can achieve – or shall we say, get away with – absolutely anything, whether I'm wearing an off-white shirt or not.

Chapter Seven – Technology and the Future of Accessible Travel

So here we are, nearing the end of my first book. What I'd like to talk about now, if you can concentrate for a little while longer, is technology, accessibility and innovation. None of the adventures I've shared with you would have been possible without the people and technology that support and enable me. When it comes to enabling technologies, my hoist, electric wheelchair and electric bed are essential bits of kit, yet without people I wouldn't be able to use any of them. In an ideal world, I would take people out of the equation altogether, though don't get me wrong, I want to keep my family and friends, but if I could get washed and dressed in the morning on my own, I'd happily forgo getting anyone else involved.

In reality, I accepted that I'll always need people to support me a long time ago, but with the rapid speed of technological advancement these days, I do wonder if life could be made easier for me, and the people that support me. Millions of people still rely on others to get them out of bed every day, and while I don't want to do people out of a job, surely things don't have to stay this way forever? Despite being thankful everyday for my electric wheelchair and the freedom that it allows me, along with all the other bits of kit that are essential in my day-to-day life, sometimes I wish people would get a wiggle on and invent capable, cheap and friendly robots already! Is that really too much to ask??

These thoughts led me to write a technological wish list in 2015, full of things I'd love to see invented, from the sublime to the slightly more ridiculous and highly unlikely. So as well as sharing some thoughts from that ever so trendy listicle, I thought it would be a good idea to introduce you to some of the technological innovations that are actually taking place. With so many crazy advances, from 3D printing, to apps and location technology, this is a very exciting time for tech, and a potentially game-changing time for disability if the right people invest enough time and money. The problem here though, is that often, disabled people are not seen as an affluent enough target market to warrant investment by the fat cats. Why invest in a state-of-the-art robot wheelchair if you don't think any disabled people will be able to afford to buy it? It is for this reason, that the advent of cheap and cost-effective 3D printing is so exciting, as it opens up real opportunities for people to create innovative and cutting-edge products that the general population can actually afford to buy.

So this chapter is a splash of dreaming, mixed with a healthy dollop of reality. With the right amount of funding, the disability sector could move forward in leaps and bounds over the next few years, and who knows, I might get that robot after all...

Come fly with me, let's fly, let's fly away

Dream – A Flying Wheelchair

You all remember the cult cartoon *Inspector Gadget*, right? Well imagine "Go, Go Gadget Wheelchair copter!" the opportunities would be endless, and certainly a lot better than the hassle of getting on a plane.

Reality – Airport Innovation

Though the reality is much less futuristic than a flying wheelchair, there have been some major innovations in the aviation sector regarding accessibility in the past few years. Here are some of my favourite.

The Aviramp

Aviramp ground support equipment is designed to help disabled people, older people and children board planes in safety and with dignity. As plane stairs are often very steep, these ramps give people the opportunity to board safely and without fear of injuring themselves. For me, it would mean I could be pushed up the ramp in a wheelchair or an airport transfer chair, as opposed to being roughly bumped up the stairs.

The Eagle Hoist

Airports around the world are finally catching on to the fact that disabled people don't want to be picked up by airport staff and carried to their seats. Many airports – including London Gatwick –

now have Eagle Hoists, hospital grade hoists that are very narrow and can therefore move safely down plane aisles, restoring dignity and improving safety.

The little boy's room

Dream – Going it alone

Whether it's holding my urine bottle, wiping my bum or helping me have a shower, I've always needed assistance in the bathroom. Far too many people have seen 'mini-me', and if there was a way of doing any of this on my own and having less people involved, I'd be a very happy guy, especially as I'd finally get to sing in the shower without troubling someone else's ears!

Reality – Small changes, big improvement

The Oasis Seated Shower System

If you've got room in your bathroom and can afford it, the Oasis Seated Shower System is designed to wash the whole body without anyone else getting involved. Once you're seated on the moveable but secure pads, jets of water and soap can be delivered to all those hard to reach areas, as the pads gently move you around. The whole system is controlled by a remote that can be operated by you or your carer, and shampoo, conditioner and soap can be fed into the system as and when required. Cool!

Clos-o-Mat Toilets

Although this also requires a bit of an outlay, Clos-o-Mat toilets really are ideal for people who are tired of having their bum wiped by another person. With an integrated bidet system, followed by warm, drying air, Clos-o-Mats provide the full service, meaning you can poo in peace! The system is operated via an elbow pad, so the majority of people with limited or very limited mobility will be able to use it.

Aquarius Portable Bidet

For those who are often on the move (like me!) an alternative to the Clos-o-Mat is the Aquarius Portable Bidet System. Coming with a carry case, the system is easy to install into any toilet and is battery operated and rechargeable. Although the Aquarius doesn't have a drying feature, it does cut down on half the work and is a hygienic alternative to toilet paper.

Go Mobility Shower Chair

Another useful travel accessory, the Go Mobility Shower Chair is a folding shower chair, which folds away into a wheelie suitcase and can therefore be wheeled around easily and discreetly. This a great alternative to having to push your shower chair around the airport, especially if the wheels are similar to those of a wonky shopping trolley!

Moving on up

Dream – Where's Wallace and Gromit when you need them?

Having to turn at night, most nights of the year, is the bane of my life, but it's even worse for my fiancé Kasia. Having to wake her up every night is not something I enjoy doing, and it's certainly not good for her health either. It would be great to be able to do this with the simple push of a button and then either have a bed that was capable of moving me, or a friendly robot that could lend me a hand. Similarly, it would be great to be able to get into my wheelchair without human assistance, and I think a Wallace and Gromit style machine would be perfect here. Support for my arms would be very welcome too. I used to be able to scratch my head by crawling my hand up my nose, something that my step-brother and cousin still recreate to amusing effect, but as my SMA has bit harder, I've become less flexible. So, wouldn't it be great if my arms were supported or my wheelchair had arms? The opportunities would be endless; I could get up to all sorts of mischief! A robot that could be my personal physiotherapist and stretch my limbs out from time to time wouldn't go amiss either!

Reality – It's not so far from the dream!

Japanese "care" robots

Japan is the technological and market leader when it comes to 'care' robots. Two different software giants have produced robots in the past few years, which have been designed to assist with care work, and they are being gradually phased into some care homes in the country to see how things go. NTT, Japan's biggest telecommunications firm, has created a small and compact robot for a relatively cheap price, that can interact with various wearable tech so that it can check your blood pressure and heart rate as well as having a somewhat robotic chat with you. On the much larger end of the scale, SoftBank have created Pepper, which the producers are hoping people will use for elderly care and even babysitting. As the bot apparently learns from listening to conversations, the possibilities are potentially endless, and with fully articulated arms, it might actually be able to do some of the things that I need, though quite where you'd store it, is another matter! Last, but by no means least, there's Robear, the project of scientist Toshiharu Mukai. Shaped like a friendly bear, Robear certainly has the strength of his ursine relatives and is capable of lifting a person from their bed and into their wheelchair, as well as helping people stand. It's all getting a bit *Terminator*, albeit in helpful bear-shaped form!

Rolling with the homies

Dream – Climbing stairs and exploring beaches

Much like the Daleks – in their original incarnation at least – stairs are my nemesis, well, stairs and vegetables. It would be fantastic if my wheelchair was capable of getting up and down stairs, and would make so many places instantly accessible – though this doesn't mean that companies would get to slack off when it comes to making their premises better equipped for disabled people! Being able to drive on different surfaces would also be a massive bonus, and getting onto sand in particular without the wheels getting ruined would be a vast improvement. Cocktail by the sea por favor!

Reality – is that a monster truck or a chair?

The life and death of the iBot

The world's first stair climbing wheelchair has sadly come and gone. It lasted five years before disappearing in a puff of expensive smoke. Sold by well-known brand Johnson & Johnson, the chair was on sale in America for a staggering $22,000, thus putting it out of the reach of most of the people who needed it. The world's first stair-climbing chair was always likely to be ludicrously expensive though, but when only a few hundred were sold each year, manufacturing the chair soon became unsustainable. With the technology now out there though, there is hope that in the future other companies will be able to manufacture similar products for a much lower price. Here's to hoping!

Sand Chairs

When it comes to rolling out onto the golden sands, Cornwall Council are doing a good job with their new manual sand chairs. These chairs have inflatable wheels, which allow them to move comfortably over sand and pebbles, so while the dream of being able to traverse the sand in my electric wheelchair is still not possible, I've high hopes that it soon will be.

3D Printing and disability

When it comes to the future of disability tech though, my highest hopes are reserved for 3D printing. Disability Horizons has already featured an interview with Standard Cyborg CEO Jeff Huber, who has been 3D printing affordable, waterproof prosthetics for the American market, and there are a whole host of other businesses that are also getting in on the game. As the technology advances and becomes more widely available, I don't think it'll be long until we've all got 3D printers in our homes and we're able to print any number of cheap gadgets to help us with our day-to-day lives. The expansion of the sharing economy means many of these blueprints will also be available for free on the Internet, and we'll even be able to design our own products and then share them with the rest of the world.

So while inviting robots into our homes might be a bit of a scary prospect, let alone an expensive one, 3D printing really will be open and accessible to all and I think it's something that we should all get behind. You never know, I might be able to 3D print my own robot one day!

So here's to the future!

CPSIA information can be obtained at www.ICGtesting.com
Printed in the USA
LVOW10s1535121016

508486LV00016B/819/P